Richmond
during the Revolution
1775–83

Richmond
during the Revolution
1775–83

Harry M. Ward and Harold E. Greer, Jr.

Published for the
Richmond Independence Bicentennial Commission

By the University Press of Virginia
Charlottesville

THE UNIVERSITY PRESS OF VIRGINIA
Copyright © 1977 by the Rector and Visitors
of the University of Virginia

First published 1977

Library of Congress Cataloging in Publication Data
Ward, Harry M
Richmond during the Revolution, 1775–83.

Bibliography: p.
Includes index.
1. Richmond—History—Revolution, 1775–1783.
I. Greer, Harold E., joint author. II. Richmond Independence Bicentennial
Commission. III. Title.
F234.R557W37   975.5'451'03   77-22586
ISBN 0-8139-0715-2

Printed in the United States of America

Contents

Illustrations

Map—Richmond today, with Revolutionary sites identified—
follows p. 3.

FOREWORD

Richmond is familiar to scholars in the field of history and government, but to others—even Richmonders—the city's development and its part in the Revolutionary War is virtually unknown. This work is designed to tell that story.

This volume is an example of the efforts of the Richmond Independence Bicentennial Commission, under whose sponsorship the book was written. The Commission was established by City Council to celebrate the birth of our country by scholarly programs and significant projects that remind us not only of the contributions and sacrifices of Richmonders during the years 1776–81, but also of the heritage and responsibilities that carry forward for the next 200 years.

We present this history, hoping it will encourage others to uncover aspects of Richmond's past. On behalf of the city of Richmond, we want to congratulate the authors, Dr. Harry M. Ward and Dr. Harold E. Greer, Jr., and the Richmond Independence Bicentennial Commission.

Hon. Thomas Bliley, Jr.
Mayor—City of Richmond
1976

Hon. Henry L. Marsh III
Mayor—City of Richmond
1977

Preface

When a Richmonder reflects on the "the war," it is likely to be the Civil War that comes to mind. Richmond's role in the Revolutionary War was also important, however, and the impact of the Revolutionary War on Richmond's future was perhaps even greater, from a long-range view, than that of the Civil War. The purpose of this book is to trace Richmond's role in the American Revolution and to reconstruct everyday life in Richmond during that time, 1775–83. The book will show how a small frontier trading town at the falls of the James became the capital of the largest of the original thirteen states and developed into a bustling community with its own city government.

Although Richmond experienced firsthand only brief contact with the enemy during the Revolution, hardly any other place can claim as direct an involvement with the war. It was in Richmond that two Virginia conventions committed the colony to revolution; the city and the immediate area became the recruiting and supply depot for the Southern Army; and the city was invaded by three British generals—Arnold, Phillips, and Cornwallis. Richmond was burned by Arnold, and Manchester—across the river and now part of Richmond—was later destroyed by Phillips. It was during this period that the capital was moved from Williamsburg; many government agencies, including the War Office of the state, were located in Richmond. The city became a detention center for loyalists. In command of Virginia forces, first Steuben and then Lafayette were frequent visitors in Richmond to consult with Virginia officials. The city and its vicinity were the sites of encampments of Continental detachments. The city even had to face a "bonus march." An understanding of the role of Richmond in the Revolution casts insights into the war in the South.

Local history can be much more than a salute to tradition and lore that have been hallmarks of local pride. Indeed, it often turns out, as in this investigation, that myths are deflated; but in the pursuit of the reality of people and conditions, to see actions in the context of human beings, with their strengths and weaknesses, there emerges an understanding of the fiber—social and individual—that left a legacy of democracy and freedom. Studying the social structure, economic life, politics, culture, and events of a populace rapidly undergoing the transition from a primitive to an urban community during a time of crisis gives a perspective to the organic community that is Richmond.

Richmond had all the characteristics of a frontier community. Not surprisingly, the first mayor of Richmond had an eye gouged out in a local tavern. The boomtown atmosphere attracted all strata of society—political leaders, merchants, craftsmen, and ne'er-do-wells. Population was mobile among all classes. As a thriving port, mercantile crossroads, seat of government, and military headquarters, Richmond presents an important facet of urban life in America during the Revolution.

The authors are grateful for the support of the Richmond Independence Bicentennial Commission and the city of Richmond that had made this book possible. Dr. Lynn Sims, the Executive Director of the Commission, helped immeasurably in the final stages prior to publication, and a special thanks goes to Mr. Donald McCammond, Chairman of the Commission, whose efforts expedited the final product. The University of Richmond aided substantially by granting a summer research fellowship. Thomas Ford of Colonial Williamsburg, Inc., had the difficult task of abridging the manuscript to one-third of its original size and rearranging and editing the final result.

Personnel of many libraries have abundantly given their time in helping to track down documents. The greatest part of the research was accomplished at the Virginia State Library, in its tremendous manuscript and microfilm collections. Mrs. Ethel M. Slonaker greatly facilitated research by arranging what seemed like an interminable number of interlibrary loans. Many persons on the staffs of the Reference Room and the Archives Division afforded invaluable aid, especially Donald Morecock, Dennis Hallerman, Daphne Gentry, William Lange, Emily Jones, William Ray, Jean Pairo, Robert Clay, Mrs. Jewell Clark, Conly Edwards, and Anthony Gonzales. To these and to Dr. Louis H. Manarin, the State Archivist, Dr. John W. Dudley, also of the Archives Division, and Milton R. Russell, head of the Reference Room, we express our appreciation. Michael Sanchez-Savaadra, formerly of the publications department of the State Library and now curator of the Valentine Museum, was an important resource person because of his expertise in Virginia military units during the Revolution; he also seemed to have x-ray vision in ferreting out manuscript items in the cellar vaults of the State Library. Murphy DeWitt Smith, Associate Librarian of the American Philosophical Society; Howson W. Cole, Waverly K. Winfree, and Virginius C. Hall of the Virginia Historical Society; and Betty Gibson and Eve Anderson of the Valentine Museum were all generous with their assistance.

Acknowledgment is given to unstinting aid provided by the staffs of The New-York Historical Society, the manuscript room of the New York Public Library, the Historical Society of Pennsylvania, the National Archives, and the manuscript division and dissertation microfilm room of the Library of Congress. Thanks are also due The New-York Historical Society for permission to quote from the Steuben Papers. Last but not least, appreciation is expressed to Laura Greer, both for allowing the intrusion of a host of early Richmonders for two years and for sharing in the typing of the manuscript.

HARRY M. WARD
HAROLD E. GREER, JR.

Richmond
during the Revolution
1775–83

Prologue

The falls of the James River made an indelible impression on John F. D. Smyth, an English traveler. When he visited Richmond a few years before the Revolution, the river's cascade hardly felt the restraints of man. As Smyth described the scene for his countrymen:

> Here a ledge of rocks interrupts the whole stream of the river, for the length of seven miles; during the course of which, that vast current of water rushes down, raging with impetuosity, tumbling and dashing from rock to rock, with an astonishing roar, that is heard for many miles distance. The land suddenly swells into hills of a great height, and abounds with prodigious rocks, and large stones as well as trees.
>
> On the summits of those hills, most of which overlook, and many of them over-hang the falling torrent of the James, handsome houses are built, which command a wild, grand, and most elegant perspective.
>
> The James, here, is about half a mile wide; the tide flows up to the very rocks of the falls, which continue to interrupt the current for the length of seven miles above.

Another traveler, Dr. Johann David Schoepf, a Hessian surgeon touring the new republic at the end of the Revolution, called the James "one of the greatest and most beautiful of American streams." At Richmond, he declared:

> ... a vast number of great and small fragments of rock fill the bed of the river as far as the eye can see, and through these the current, with foaming uproar, makes its way. What with the help of devious banks and the forest on both sides, the impression from a view of the whole is great and pleasing. The noise of the falls, especially at night, is heard not only throughout the town but, before the wind, for several miles around.

In 1678 William Byrd I, recognizing this location as a likely site for a trading post and water mills, obtained a tract of land at the falls of the James River. His grant included an area five miles long and two miles deep on the north side of the river, one mile deep on the south side. His son, William Byrd II, inherited the land.

By the 1730s, prospering warehouses, a store, and at least one tavern stood near the falls. A ferry provided transportation across the river. Commercial and trading interests of the region, converging here, created a center of population. Byrd decided to set up a town at the falls and assigned Major William Mayo to survey a portion of the land for that purpose.

Mayo completed his task in 1737, a survey of the area that today extends from Seventeenth Street to Twenty-fifth Street, the numbered streets running north and south. East-west streets were then what are today—Cary, Main, Franklin, Grace, and Broad. The streets were to be sixty-five feet wide, forming thirty-two squares, each containing four lots. Within three years, the purchaser of a lot was to build a house at least twenty-four feet by sixteen feet, fronting within five feet of the street. Byrd named the town Richmond because it resembled Richmond on the Thames in Surrey County, England.

In May 1742, with approximately 250 people living in the town drawn off east of Shockoe Creek, John Coles presented a petition to the General Assembly that the town of Richmond be legally constituted. Most of the lots in the town had been built on, and Byrd planned to lay out additional lots in the adjoining areas.

The General Assembly, recognizing the significance of the growing town, "at the uppermost landing on the river, where the public warehouses are built," declared the town of Richmond in Henrico County established. The lands between the town and the river and between the town and Shockoe Creek—donated by Byrd as a common—were confirmed as town property, and the Assembly also decreed annual fair days for Richmond. Two-day fairs were to be held on the second Thursday and Friday in May and the second Thursday and Friday in November for the sale of "all manner of cattle, victuals, provisions, goods, wares and merchandises whatsoever."

Being legally constituted a town did little to set Richmond apart from Henrico County. The county court still served as the town's governing body, and the county sheriff, as its law enforcement officer. As before, the citizens of Richmond petitioned the General Assembly directly about some of the town's problems. In response to one such petition, in 1752 the General Assembly appointed nine trustees of the town: Peter Randolph, William Byrd III, William Randolph, Bowler Cocke (the younger), Richard Randolph, Thomas Atchison, Samuel Gleadowe, Samuel DuVal, and John Pleasants.

For some fifteen years these men formed the town's sole approach to self-rule. And a very tentative one it was, their powers being limited to regulating the "orderly building of the houses," the laying out of new streets, and the bounding of lots.

In time, the third William Byrd, faced with financial problems, assigned his land in the Richmond area to a group of men who were to assist him in paying his debts. These men decided in 1768 to sell the property by lottery, a popular method at that time. They divided Byrd's holdings into 839 prizes—to be offered with 9,161 blanks, totaling 10,000 lottery tickets, each selling for £5.

The town of Shockoe, west of Richmond, and the town of Rocky Ridge, across the river, were included in the lottery. Prizes included land as far west as what is today the corner of River Road and Three Chopt Road in West Richmond. Among the lucky ticket holders was George Washington. Some winners did not claim their prizes at the time and others never did, resulting in title disputes later.

By 1769, Richmond had grown to a population of 574, and it was ready to annex part of the area in the Byrd lottery. An appeal to the General Assembly resulted in the addition of the "place called Shoccoes," continuing as far west as what is today Foushee Street. The part of the lottery laid off as Rocky Ridge—and later to become a part of Richmond—was established as the town of Manchester.

By 1773, only three of the trustees appointed in 1752 were still living. Also, the legality of the election of other trustees had been questioned. And in any case, the powers of the board of trustees needed to be expanded. On petition from the citizens of the town, the General Assembly appointed Richard Adams, Robert Brown, George Donald, Turner Southall, Patrick Coutts, Archibald Bryce, William Randolph, James Buchanan, William Byrd III, Richard Randolph, and Samuel DuVal as trustees.

Richmond Today, with Revolutionary Sites Identified

A. Henrico County Courthouse (also used by Richmond)
B. Henrico County Jail (also served as Richmond jail and state public jail)
C. Old Capitol Building
D. Thomas Jefferson's residence when he was governor, at the center of Shockoe Hill (approximate location)
E. Benjamin Harrison's residence when he was governor (approximate location)
F. Council of State meeting place
G. Gallows where state criminals were hung
H. Byrd tobacco inspection warehouse
I. Byrd's second tobacco inspection warehouse
J. Shockoe tobacco inspection warehouse
K. Shockoe second tobacco inspection warehouse
L. Shockoe landing, used by the Shockoe and Byrd tobacco inspection warehouses and as a landing for the ferry to Manchester (at the time of the Revolution no island hindered direct travel to the south side of the James River from this landing)

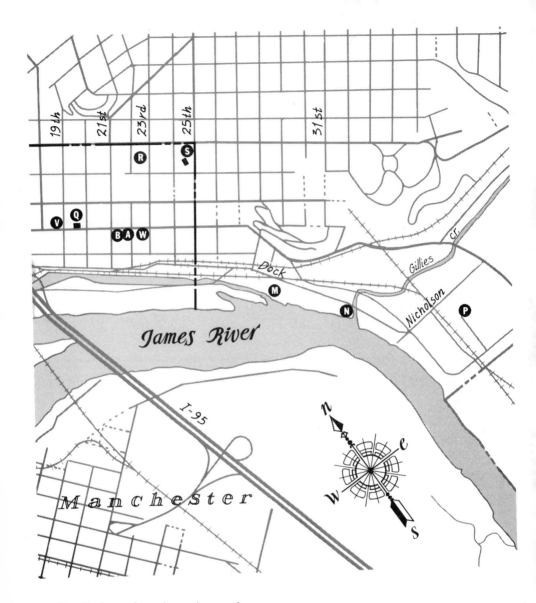

M.   Rocketts tobacco inspection warehouse
N.   Rocketts landing, used by Rocketts tobacco inspection warehouse
O.   City Market
P.   Richmond Ropewalk
Q.   Old Stone House
R.   Richard Adams House, located on Richmond Hill (now Church Hill)
S.   St. John's Church
T.   Belvidere
U.   Serafino Formicola's tavern (exact location between 15th and 17th streets is not known
V.   Gabriel Galt's tavern
W.   Abraham Cowley's tavern, founded in 1737, run in the war years by Stephen Tankard
X.   Richard Hogg's tavern
———··———Boundary of the city of Richmond in 1782, according to the Richmond tax list

(Map by Paul Nickerson.)

The specific power granted the trustees reflected Richmond's increasing importance as a trade center: "to meet as often as they shall think necessary for appointing a public quay, and such places upon the river for public landings as they shall think most convenient, and if the same shall be necessary, shall direct the making of wharfs and cranes at such public landings for the public use." The trustees also received power to establish rules for placing houses and for repairing and changing streets, landings, and wharfs. They retained the power to fill vacancies among themselves.

The General Assembly acted on a number of local Richmond problems in 1773. It again declared unlawful the erection of wooden chimneys in the town. It enacted a law forbidding any person, after January 20, 1774, to allow his swine or goats to run at large in the town. An animal in violation of this law could be killed, but the person who killed it must notify the owner or—if the owner was not known—a justice of the peace, who would assign the animal to the use of the poor.

In the years before the Revolution, therefore, Richmond was a town whose only governing body had only specific, limited powers granted by the Assembly. The citizens had no voice in choosing their trustees. The Henrico County Court exercised real local authority. This condition existed through the opening years of the Revolution, until the General Assembly established a city government in Richmond in 1782.

CHAPTER ONE

Richmond on the Eve
of the Revolution

AS THE REVOLUTION approached, Richmond was little more than a village of muddy streets and small frame houses. It did have a church, warehouses for tobacco and other trade goods, taverns, and a small courthouse. No doubt there was also a full complement of stables, privies, and other amenities of civilization at that time.

Main Street, east of Shockoe Creek, was Richmond's major thoroughfare in the time of the Revolution. Along it stood the Henrico courthouse, Henrico County jail, market, Galt's Tavern, and Cowley's Tavern (referred to as Tankard's Ordinary during the war), as well as the shops of some of the city's barbers, tailors, and craftsmen. Across Shockoe Creek to the west, other taverns and Byrd's warehouse fronted on Main Street. Shockoe Hill, future site of the capitol and the public square, was approached by what is today Thirteenth Street, (which becomes Governor Street one block north of Main Street) supposedly following an old Indian trail. Twenty-fifth Street gave principal access to what is today Church Hill.

Roads led out of Richmond to Williamsburg on the east, to Hanover Town and Fredericksburg on the north, to Westham and Charlottesville on the west, and to Petersburg on the south. To Williamsburg, a two-day journey, the road past Bottoms Bridge and New Kent Court House was described by the traveler Schoepf as being "mainly through gloomy forest, only here and there tilled land or a wretched cabin."

The distance between Richmond and Williamsburg could also be traveled by boat on the James River. One such traveler, shortly before the Revolution, wrote of hiring a boat and four Negroes for a dollar and a half a day for the trip. The group left Williamsburg on August 9 and arrived in Richmond on August 11, sleeping on the boat on the way.

Reuben Coutts operated the James River ferry to Manchester. From Shockoe landing, between Fifteenth and Seventeenth streets, it crossed just below, and parallel to, what

is today the Fourteenth Street Bridge. The marquis de Chastellux, who used this ferry, described it as being a short passage
and having two boats to accommodate travelers.

The population in 1775 can be roughly calculated, but the
figures are far from certain. As we have seen, the town
contained about 250 inhabitants in 1742 and 574 in 1769, a
growth of twelve persons per year for those twenty-seven years.
Extending that rate for another six years would make a total
population of 646 souls.

A census taken in 1782 counted 1,031 persons living in the
town. At least 43 percent of those households had not been established in Richmond two years earlier, however, when the
capital was moved from Williamsburg. That would suggest a
population of only 587 as late as 1779. The rough calculation,
then, gives a town of somewhere around 600 men, women, and
children just before the Revolution.

On the assumption that population elements would have
been about the same in 1775 as they were in 1782, we can say
that men outnumbered women (about three to two), whites outnumbered blacks (about eleven to nine), and the accent was
strongly on youth.

Among the slightly over five hundred whites on the 1782 tax
list thirty-four percent were children of fifteen or younger,
forty-four percent fell in the age span from sixteen through
thirty, and only about one person in five had passed his or her
thirty-first birthday. The census takers didn't give the ages of
slaves, but among the free blacks whose ages were listed in the
tax list, forty-three percent were under age fifteen, twenty-
eight and a half percent were between sixteen and thirty, and
twenty-eight and a half percent were thirty-one or older.

Blacks and whites lived close together, too. Of the 1,031
people in Richmond in 1782—when the list of inhabitants was
made—468, or forty-five percent, were blacks. By far the
largest portion of these were slaves. However, a significant
number, 40 of the 468, were free blacks. Nineteen slaves lived
on their own, allowed by their masters to hire themselves out,
returning to their owners a portion or all of their earnings.

Blacks lived in all areas of the city. There was no pattern of
housing discrimination in revolutionary Richmond. Free blacks
and slaves who hired themselves out lived in each of the four

wards in general proportion to the number of whites in that ward. Neither were they relegated to any one area within the ward, and blacks and whites often had dwellings on the same lot.

The 1782 tax list provides information about some kinds of property owned by the 138 households. Eighty-seven households owned slaves, the majority owning only one to four. Four households had more than fifteen slaves: Richard Hogg, who owned a large tavern, owned eighteen, and Serafino Formicola, also a tavern owner, seventeen. Richard Adams owned eighteen slaves, and Governor Harrison listed sixteen slaves in Richmond.

Forty-five households owned cattle. Slightly more than half, twenty-seven households, had one or two cows, while only five households owned five or more. A larger number of households, seventy-three, owned horses. Thirty-one of these owned one horse; fifteen owned two horses; nineteen owned three to five horses; and eight owned six to nine horses.

Free Negroes owned some property in the city and paid taxes. Mary Lucas owned three cows, five horses, a four-wheel carriage, and a wagon. Brazil de Romo and his wife, Hannah, had a horse and a mare; Humphrey and Nancy Baine, a horse; Kate Burcher (Robertson), a horse. James and Molly Norman seem to have owned part of lot no. 71.

According to the 1782 assessment on property, the ownership of lots and buildings within the city was widely distributed. With the exceptions of Richard Adams, who owned lots with buildings and fifteen unimproved lots on Church Hill (the area where St. John's Church is located), and James Buchanan, who alone or jointly owned forty-two unimproved lots in the western part of the city, no citizen of Richmond had large property holdings within the boundaries of the city. Many lots remained unclaimed, and it was fairly easy to purchase real estate in the city. All lots measured one-half acre, and some were valued as low as £5, the cost of a ticket in the original lottery.

Schoepf described the houses in Richmond in 1783 as "almost wholly of wood and scattered irregularly on two heights, divided by the Shokoes, a small brook; the number of them is not large nor are they in themselves of a handsome appearance." Jefferson's slave Isaac remembered all the houses except two being wood in 1780. Houses listed in the paper for sale or rent in Richmond during the revolutionary years usually included a garden and such separate outhouses as kitchens and smokehouses.

Only one house that was in Richmond during the time of the Revolution is still standing, the Old Stone House on the north side of Main Street between Nineteenth and Twentieth streets (see fig. 1). During the Revolution the house belonged to Samuel Ege.

The homes of Richard Adams and Col. William Byrd impressed J. F. D. Smyth during his tour of the United States in 1769. "The most commanding and excellent situations above Richmond are," he wrote, "the seat of a Mr. Adams, on the

Fig. 1. Old Stone House. Believed to have been constructed in the late 1730s, this is the only residence in Richmond during the revolutionary war that still stands today. (Courtesy of the Virginia State Library.)

summit of the hill which over-looks the town; and Belvidera, an elegant villa belonging to the late Colonel William Byrd. . . ."

The Adams house probably stood on the block in Church Hill bounded by Broad, Grace, Twenty-second, and Twenty-third streets. Belvidere (not within the boundaries of Richmond at that time) was built by William Byrd III, probably in the 1750s, in the center of the area in Oregon Hill bounded today by Belvidere, Laurel, China, and Holly streets.

Six other prominent houses in the Richmond area during the Revolution were Ampthill, home of Archibald Cary; Wilton, home of William Randolph; Powhatan Seat, built by Joseph Mayo; Mount Comfort, home of Samuel DuVal; Windsor, owned by Daniel Hylton; and Tuckahoe, owned by Thomas Randolph.

The marquis de Chastellux, an officer in Rochambeau's army, observed several "superb" houses in the Warwick neighborhood, and especially singled out Archibald Cary's home, Ampthill (see fig. 2). Just across the river from Ampthill, on the north bank six miles below Richmond was Wilton, a large Georgian-style house sixty feet long and forty-six feet wide (see fig. 3). Powhatan Seat was built between 1726 and 1732 on what is now known as Fulton Hill, the traditional site of Powhatan's Indian village. A handsome brick structure, two stories high with a basement, the house took the shape of the letter *T*, with the main part sixty by twenty-four feet, and the wing behind it thirty-six by twenty feet. The house included a winding stairway.

Mount Comfort stood north of Richmond on a four hundred acre estate bordering Shockoe Creek, later designated as the Chestnut Hill and Highland Park sections of Richmond. Mount Comfort, built by 1748, was reported to be the first brick residence in the vicinity and a major social center for the area.

Windsor stood near the river in the area that is today Windsor Farms, named after it. Tuckahoe, built adjacent to Tuckahoe Creek, overlooked the James River. Lt. Thomas Anburey, a captured British officer on parole who stayed at Tuckahoe, briefly described it this way: "It is in the form of an H, and has the appearance of two houses, joined by a large saloon; each wing has two stories, and four large rooms on a floor. . . ."

Fig. 2. Ampthill. First located in Chesterfield County downstream from Richmond on the south side of the James River at the village of Warwick, Ampthill was moved to the west end of Richmond in 1929. It was built about 1730 by Henry Cary II, and at the time of the Revolution was the residence of Archibald Cary, a leader of the patriot party in Virginia. Above is the exterior of Ampthill after it was moved. At left is an interior view before Ampthill was moved. (Courtesy of the Virginia State Library.)

Fig. 3.   Wilton. Constructed in about 1750 by William Randolph III a few miles below Richmond on the north bank of the James River, Wilton was moved to the west end of Richmond in 1933. (Courtesy of the Virginia State Library.)

Little concrete evidence survives on which to base a discussion of education in Richmond in the time of the Revolution. Public documents, petitions, and wills indicate that most who subscribed to these instruments could sign their own names. Women were less likely to be able to write than were men.

Some of the wealthier citizens sent their children to England for schooling. Joshua Storrs specified in his will that his son Gervas was to be sent to relatives in England "in order that he may be well educated." Others may have been taught by their parents, or by persons employed for that purpose by a family or group of families. Still others attended, at some stage in their education, the College of William and Mary.

Julia Wheatley announced in January 1776, after the burning of Norfolk, that she was moving to Richmond with her daughter, who would open a boarding school for young ladies in her home. The students were to be taught reading, writing, arithmetic, the French language, and various kinds of needle-work. The school may not have been successful, for in October 1777 the Wheatleys gave notice that they were leaving Rich-mond.

In the meantime, Miles Taylor advertised in the *Virginia Gazette* in July 1777 for a schoolmaster for the town of Rich-mond. Taylor promised that "any person who can bring with him proper testimonials of his capacity, diligence, and good morals, will have very great encouragement." The tax census of 1782 listed Thomas Omohundro as schoolmaster and as having been in Richmond for eighteen months. He resided at the northwest corner of Franklin and Eighteenth streets.

When the Revolution broke out, the only church having a building or a meeting place in Richmond was the established church, the Church of England. This church, today known as St. John's, was one of four churches in Henrico Parish, an area identical in area with Henrico County. Not all the records of the parish during the time of the Revolution survive, but it is known that Miles Selden, Jr., served as rector of Henrico Parish from 1752 until 1785.

Although a clergyman in the Church of England, Selden strongly supported the patriot cause. He was elected chairman of the Henrico County Committee of Safety, chaplain of the Virginia Conventions of March and July-August 1775, and chaplain of the General Assembly in 1780. He conducted thanksgiving services at St. John's after the victory at Yorktown.

Baptists appeared in Richmond during the Revolution. Elijah Baker of Lunenburg County was baptized in 1769 and then spread his faith from Henrico County to the Eastern Shore. Fourteen Baptists organized a church in June 1780 in the home of John Franklin at the corner of what are today Car-rington and Pink streets. Though the church met in homes and did not have a building during the Revolution, it became the first church in Richmond to have a resident pastor when Joshua Morris purchased a lot on the south side of Main Street at the corner of Second Street in July 1783 and built a house there. Morris served this church—which evolved into the First Baptist

Church—until 1786, when he joined the migration west to Kentucky. Baptist members came often from the poorer classes and included slaves as "brothers" and "sisters" in their church community. Minutes were not kept by the church, and little is known about the membership.

Quakers also were active in Henrico County. The White Oak Swamp congregation, which had Richmond members, was the one church in or near the town whose minutes survive. The church minutes reported that "Love and Unity are pretty well maintained" and "Friends are generally careful to avoid vain Sports, places of diversion, the unnecessary frequenting of Taverns and Intemperance." Yet they were concerned that "true plainness" was "too much deviated from by some of the youth, both in speech and deportment."

Besides Baptists and Quakers, another dissenter group in Henrico County at the time of the Revolution were the Anabaptists. John Lindsey presented to the Henrico County Court a recommendation from two elders that he was a proper person to be licensed as an Anabaptist preacher in the county. He received a license to perform marriages.

There were five Jews living in Richmond during the Revolution. Four appeared on the tax list compiled in 1782: Isaiah Isaacs and his wife, Mary, Jacob I. Cohen, and Jacob Mordecai. The three men were listed as merchants. Marcus Elcan's name appears as a witness to a deed in 1782. Two years later he is referred to in the records as a merchant. The Jewish chemist, Jacob Rubsamen, lived in Manchester at the time. Within less than ten years, twenty-nine heads of families were mentioned in the membership of the congregation Beth Shalome.

The period of the Revolution was a time of struggle by dissenter groups in Richmond and throughout the state. Baptists, Quakers, and Anabaptists such as the Mennonites, as well as other groups like the Presbyterians, sought to disestablish the Church of England and to allow full religious freedom to all groups. Jefferson estimated that two-thirds of the people of Virginia had become dissenters by the beginning of the Revolution.

For information on how Richmonders earned their livings on the eve of the Revolution, we must again look backward from the census of 1782. Of the 147 people listing occupations on the tax list, the largest number, 36, were merchants, including shopkeepers and peddlers. Nineteen made their living from carpentry or building skills, while 22 more used other craft skills. Eighteen were involved in making clothing and shoes. Four were printers; 5 were barbers; 1 was a chemist; 1, a schoolmaster; and 1 an attorney. Seven worked as wagoners and 7 were laborers of various titles. Two were listed as planters. Eleven worked in some way at taverns or a boarding house, and 9 worked for the state—from the keeper of the public jail to the governor himself.

The occupations of the free blacks is not given in the tax records, and only a few are known. Abraham, was a fireman at Westham Foundry (seven miles upriver, on the north bank, from Richmond). Several of the women were household or kitchen servants, sometimes living with a white family: Kate Bilberry worked for Robert Baine, Sal for Samuel Ege, and Betty for Miles Taylor. Kate Burcher, listed on the tax list as Kate Robertson, wife of Peter Robertson, earned a livelihood by running a "disorderly house." Others no doubt worked as laborers at whatever jobs were available. Some may have been skilled workers in crafts or industries.

Four men appeared as doctors in the tax list of 1782. They were Robert Brown, Andrew Leiper, James Currie, and William Foushee—who had been in Richmond five years. Dr. Brown's training and background are not known. By 1772 he was practicing in Richmond, for he advertised medicine for sale at his shop there. He was appointed by the House of Burgesses in 1776 to serve on a committee to determine the efficacy of a cancer cure. In 1776 he supplied medicine for the army.

Dr. Andrew Leiper, born in 1717, studied medicine in Philadelphia, then practiced in Richmond. He was the medical instructor of William Henry Harrison, who later became president. Leiper served as quarantine physician at the port of Richmond and was treating people with yellow fever there when he died in 1798. He is buried in St. John's cemetery.

Dr. James Currie was one of Richmond's leading physicians both before and after the Revolution. Born at Annandale, Scotland, in 1745, he moved to Virginia in his youth. He got his training, however, at Edinburgh. By 1772 Dr. Currie operated an apothecary shop in Richmond. He advertised in the *Virginia*

Gazette in 1779 that despite inflation "my fees for the practice of PHYSICK, from the beginning of this year, 1779, will be at the old rates (such as I charged before the exorbitant prices of medicines, as well as every necessary of life and article of commerce, made it highly requisite and strictly equitable to raise them). . . ." In 1782 Thomas Jefferson took his two oldest girls to Archibald Cary's home at Ampthill to have them inoculated for smallpox by Dr. Currie.

Dr. William Foushee (see fig. 4) was born into a Huguenot family in the Northern Neck. Educated at Edinburgh, he first practiced medicine in Norfolk, then moved to Richmond in 1777. Foushee also advertised in 1779 that he was still charging the same prices, despite inflation: five shillings for a visit in town in the daytime. In payment, he would accept commodities as well as cash and tobacco. He expected to be paid at the time

Fig. 4. William Foushee. A prominent Richmond physician, Foushee was elected the city's first mayor in 1782. (Courtesy of the Virginia State Library.)

he rendered services. However, he added this note: "The above has not in view the indigent, or those whose circumstances may render it necessary to make an abatement, they will be attended as formerly."

Among others who advertised their medical skills was Julia Wheatley, midwife, who moved from Norfolk to Richmond with her daughter, the schoolteacher, in 1776 and announced that she would continue her business in Richmond. She professed her ability to cure ringworm and other disorders of both sexes. However, she stayed in Richmond only until 1777.

The tax list of 1782 named only four women as breadwinning heads of families. This is not to say that they had lived in Richmond and had been so employed since 1776. But all four engaged in occupations considered appropriate for women at the time. Sarah Hubbard, age forty and the mother of two children, worked as a washerwoman and seamstress. Mary Warrick, age forty and with five children, was also a seamstress, as was Elizabeth Oglesvey, age thirty-four and with four children. Jane Allegre, a mantua-maker, was forty-two years old and had three children. Her daughters, age eighteen and sixteen, also listed their occupation as mantua-maker.

The poor and their problems appear in the records of revolutionary Richmond in general, rather than specific, terms. Proceeds of fines specified by local ordinances were usually designated for the poor or could be appropriated for their benefit. Wood offered for sale that did not meet regulations or any goods offered for sale using false weights or measures were to be forfeited for the use of the poor. In meting out punishment for violations, poor people who could not pay fines were subject to specified numbers of lashes.

A letter from a Henrico gentleman to a friend in Williamsburg, written in 1775 when salt was in short supply and uplanders were raiding the Richmond area for salt, provides some insight into the habits and diet of the poorer people. ". . . more salt is necessary in the families of the poor and middling sort of people in this part of the country, than in the upper part, for they not having it in their power to raise pork and beef, are obliged to live upon salted fish. . . . If our poor have not salt enough to cure their fish, they must eat bread alone, because they cannot raise meat, and have not money to buy it. . . ."

Citizens in all walks of life took part in the political, as well as the economic, and social life of the city during the revolutionary period. Richmond did not have a small elite class of people who held all the powers in the city. However, several men were especially prominent, important, and influential for various reasons.

Richard Adams, who owned much of the best property on Church Hill, had been important in town life since the 1760s. Fifty years old in 1776, Adams was one of the oldest citizens. He had married Elizabeth Griffin in the 1750s, and they had ten children, one of Richmond's largest families.

Dr. William Foushee, among the most active men in public affairs, was twenty-six years old when he came to the city. Only five years later, in 1782, he was elected Richmond's first mayor. He owned an unimproved lot near Shockoe landing, probably a business investment.

Richmonders held Isaac Younghusband in high esteem, giving him the largest number of votes in the Common Hall election of 1782. He owned a store and six lots with buildings in a choice location near Galt's Tavern on Main Street. He and his wife did not live together, and he disinherited her in his will for being unfaithful to him.

The merchant James Buchanan was also active in Richmond public affairs. Elected to the first Common Hall, he served both as common councilman and as alderman and justice on the Richmond hustings court as well. One of Buchanan's most important public responsibilities was as head of the Directors of the Public Buildings in Richmond.

John Beckley provides an example of the social mobility that was possible in revolutionary Richmond. Beckley came from England at age eleven as an indentured servant of the clerk of Gloucester County. He became clerk of the Henrico Committee of Safety in 1775 and assistant clerk of the Virginia Committee of Safety in 1776. In Richmond, Beckley established a new chapter of Phi Beta Kappa, of which he had been an active member in Williamsburg. In addition to his other duties in Richmond, he practiced law and was the only person on the tax list in 1782 who listed his occupation as attorney. Beckley was elected to the Common Hall in 1782 and served as alderman and as justice on the Richmond hustings court. At the end of Foushee's term, Beckley, only twenty-six and single, became

Richmond's second mayor. Beckley later served as clerk of the United States House of Representatives and as the first Librarian of Congress.

Clearly Richmond was a place of opportunity during the Revolution. There was no overpowering aristocracy. Land could be bought easily. With a skill or with ability, one could prosper. Richmond attracted people rapidly after 1780, especially young single men. People came seeking opportunity to make a name or a fortune, and many were not disappointed.

CHAPTER TWO

The View from Church Hill— Independence

THE SPARK that eventually burst into the flame of rebellion began in Virginia as early as 1752. The citizens of Henrico took the lead, along with those of some other Virginia counties, in petitioning against the Pistole Fee. The controversy concerned the question of whether Governor Dinwiddie, the king's representative, could levy and collect a fee that the House of Burgesses, representing the people, had not authorized.

Then, early in 1768, residents of Henrico County sent a petition to the House of Burgesses declaring that Parliament had no right to suspend the New York legislature. Moreover, they said, the taxes imposed by the Townshend Act infringed on the rights and privileges of free citizens. And finally, they boldly asserted that they owed allegiance only to the crown, not to Parliament. Several other counties did much the same.

After deliberation, the burgesses adopted resolutions of their own along the lines of the county petitions and forwarded them to both houses of Parliament. With the House of Burgesses continuing to protest, Governor Botetourt dissolved it in May 1769. Following the action of other colonies, the legislators reconvened on their own authority in 1770, an act that approached rebellion. They proceeded to establish an "association" among leading merchants to prevent importation of British goods. To what extent merchants and residents in Richmond and in Henrico County supported nonimportation is not known, but presumably they cooperated with other port communities. When Parliament removed most of the Townshend duties in early 1770, nonimportation died out.

The years 1770–73 were relatively quiet in Virginia. The Tea Act of 1773 and the Coercive Acts of 1774, however, lighted the fires anew. Virginians immediately identified themselves with the oppressed colonists in New England.

A group of "the Loyal and Patriotick People" of Henrico County met at the courthouse in Richmond on July 15, 1774, and drew up an "Address" to the two burgesses of the county,

Richard Adams and Samuel DuVal. "A great number of freeholders" affixed their signatures to the document.

The address opened with Henricoans accepting the cause of Boston and New England as their own. The two burgesses were instructed "to use your best endeavours," at a convention already scheduled for August at Williamsburg, to avert certain calamities: taxation by Parliament; the trampling of "charter rights" and Parliament's changing of government in Massachusetts; and the Administration of Justice Act, which provided for "subjects to be seized and transported beyond sea to be tried for supposed offences here."

The petitioners recommended "that a General Association between all the *American* Colonies, ought immediately be entered into," to prevent importation of British goods. They proposed that it should last until Great Britain rescinded the Coercive Acts. But, they said, significantly, "the tender regard we have for our friends the merchants and manufacturers of *Great Britain,* to whom we are indebted, and who must, of course, suffer in the common cause, prevents our recommending the stopping our exports at this time." In the future, however, "we will heartily concur with the other counties of this Colony to stop all exports as well as imports, to and from Great Britain. . . ."

The first Virginia Convention met at Williamsburg, August 1–6, 1774. Richard Adams and Samuel DuVal represented Henrico County; Archibald Cary and Benjamin Watkins, Chesterfield County; and John Syme and Patrick Henry, Hanover County.

The convention went on record for renewing the "association"—nonimportation of slaves and tea and nonexportation of tobacco to begin August 10, 1775—"unless American Grievances are redressed." It chose a delegation of seven of its members to represent the colony in the soon-to-be convened Continental Congress.

Before adjourning, the delegates empowered Peyton Randolph, president of the convention, to decide on the next meeting. On January 28, 1775, the *Virginia Gazette* carried a notice for reconvening at Richmond on March 20, 1775.

The second Virginia Convention would meet in St. John's Church, a small, white-frame building perched on Richmond Hill (see fig. 5). Built in 1741, the original frame building

Fig. 5.   St. John's Church, as it was when Patrick Henry made his "liberty or death" speech. This church was also the site of the second and third Virginia Conventions in 1775. (Courtesy of the Virginia State Library.)

measured sixty-five feet in length, twenty-five feet wide, and fourteen feet high. The vestry had voted to enlarge the church in 1772 with an addition forty feet by twenty-five feet. St. John's was the largest building in Richmond. Even so, it could barely pack in the 120 delegates.

Richmond, however, was a well-chosen site. Fifty miles inland from Williamsburg, the little village symbolized an appeal to all sections of the colony. More importantly, if the governor should decide to move against the convention and arrest its leaders, there would be sufficient warning to escape.

The men who occupied the pews in St. John's Church (see fig. 6) for this decisive week in March were men of tried political experience. Most had ample service in the House of Burgesses. The ten most active delegates in the convention had each averaged over twenty years of legislative duty. All the delegates from Henrico, Chesterfield, and Hanover counties had been burgesses. Men such as Jefferson, Washington, and Mason had given much thought and preparation to the revolutionary movement.

A cordiality seemed to prevail among former factions.

Fig. 6.   Interior view of St. John's Church, as it was when Patrick Henry gave his "liberty or death" speech. (Courtesy of the Virginia State Library.)

Patrick Henry, a leader of the "Qo'hees" (up-country) and Richard Henry Lee of the tidewater "Tuckahoes"—historically the two broad sectional divisions in the House of Burgesses—were already mending their differences.

Not long after sunup on Monday, March 20, men on horseback and in gigs and carriages could be seen fording Shockoe Creek and moving up the wooded hill to the little church. A quorum quickly formed, and the convention unanimously elected Peyton Randolph as its president and a nondelegate, John Tazewell, as clerk.

The only other actions of the day were to adopt the rules of the House of Burgesses, to put the proceedings of the Continental Congress before the convention, and to invite the rector of the church, Reverend Miles Selden, Jr., to read prayers every morning of the session at nine o'clock. The convention scheduled itself to come to order at ten o'clock.

Tuesday morning the rest of the delegates appeared. A light snow was falling when Patrick Henry left Scotchtown, but when he reached St. John's the day had cleared. With new delegates straggling in, however, the convention did not settle down to serious business. Probably the delegates used most of the day in renewing acquaintances and sounding out each others' views.

On Wednesday, after discussing the proceedings of the Continental Congress, the delegates resolved to give the Congress the "warmest thanks" of Virginians. They endorsed the acts of the Congress: a letter to General Gage asking him to discontinue fortifications in Boston; a declaration of rights; approval of the Continental Association for nonexportation, nonconsumption, and nonimportation; and addresses to the king, to the people of Great Britain, to the inhabitants of St. John, Nova Scotia, Georgia, East and West Florida, and Quebec. The congressional delegates from Virginia—Richard Henry Lee, George Washington (see fig. 7), Peyton Randolph (see fig. 8), Patrick Henry, Richard Bland, Benjamin Harrison, and Edmund Pendleton (see fig. 8)—were singled out for praise.

On Thursday, the twenty-third, Edmund Pendleton (see fig. 9) proposed the first order of business: consideration of a petition of the Assembly of Jamaica to the king. The Jamaicans acknowledged that colonial rights came from the king, and they disavowed any intention of resistance to Great Britain. But the general tenor of their petition was that British policy was aimed at enslaving the colonists.

Resolutions were placed on the floor, and a debate ensued. Moderates thought the resolutions a sufficient expression of support for the Jamaicans while at the same time not condoning their political theories. Patrick Henry undoubtedly regarded the petition as incompatible with the American cause.

Sitting in pew forty-seven, near the east transcept and the nave, Henry rose and sought recognition from Randolph. He placed before the convention resolutions calling for putting the colony into a state of defense, which the clerk read:

That a well regulated Militia, composed of gentlemen and yeomen, is the natural strength, and only security of a free Government; that such a Militia in this Colony would for ever render it unnecessary for the Mother Country to keep among us, for the purpose of our defence, any Standing Army of mercenary forces, always subversive of the quiet, and dangerous to the liberties of the people, and would obviate the pretext of taxing us for their support.

That the establishment of such a Militia is at this time peculiarly

Fig. 7.   Houdon's world-famous statue of George Washington, located in the Virginia State Capitol. (Courtesy of the Virginia State Library.)

Fig. 8. Peyton Randolph. Randolph served as president of the Virginia Convention and president of the Continental Congress. (Courtesy of the Virginia Historical Society.)

Fig. 9. Edmund Pendleton. Pendleton succeeded Peyton Randolph as president of the Virginia Convention and president of the Virginia Committee of Safety. (Courtesy of the Virginia State Library.)

Fig. 10 Edmund Randolph. Randolph was Virginia Attorney General during the Revolution when Richmond was the capital. (Courtesy of the National Archives.)

Fig. 11. John Marshall. Marshall served in the Virginia Legislature during the latter part of the Revolution and stayed in Richmond to become one of her most prominent citizens. (Courtesy of National Archives.)

necessary, by the state of our laws for the protection and defence of the Country, some of which have already expired, and others will shortly do so; and that the known remissness of Government, in calling us together in a legislative capacity, renders it too insecure, in this time of danger and distress, to rely, that opportunity will be given of renewing them in General Assembly, or making any provision to secure our inestimable rights and liberties from those further violations with which they are threatened.

Henry's resolutions were not radical. Many counties had begun military preparations, and a general feeling prevailed that a call to arms would eventually be needed. The resolutions provided merely for a restoration of the militia system.

The debate, however, soon grew heated. The merits of the militia resolutions were lost in the implications of rebellion if the convention—instead of, properly, the House of Burgesses—enacted a militia bill. Henry and his followers were thought to be ready to create a separate government. Conservatives, such as Richard Bland, Benjamin Harrison, Edmund Pendleton, and Robert Carter Nicholas opposed any action that might deepen the crisis. They felt that economic sanctions would bring Great Britain to terms. To their minds, the convention should not go out on a limb while the colony lacked the means of defending itself.

A number of delegates spoke in support of Henry's resolutions. Among these was Jefferson, who, Edmund Randolph (see fig. 10) says, "argued closely, profoundly, and warmly." Thomas Nelson called God as his witness that if British troops landed in his county he would take the militia and fight them at the water's edge. He was "more than ordinarily excited. His example told those who were happy in ease and wealth that to shrink was to be dishonored." Richard Henry Lee, who had seconded Henry's resolutions, would take the floor again after Henry's famous speech.

Henry rose and received recognition from the chair. He began speaking calmly and slowly, his piercing eyes fixed toward Randolph. But all the while, contempt for the caution of the less volatile spirits was gnawing within him. His voice became louder. "There is no longer any room for hope. . . . We must fight! . . . We must fight!"

Then, in more subdued tones, Henry gave assurance that

Virginians were not alone in preparing for war and that they
had the advantage of a just cause. The peroration came like a
roll of thunder, concluding with: "I know not what course
others may take; but as for me, give me liberty or give me
death!"

We have only William Wirt's fictitious version of Henry's
speech, constructed a generation after the fact (and a decade
after Henry's death). Wirt had only the scanty recollections of
two witnesses, John Tyler (a delegate) and St. George Tucker (a
spectator). The only certainty about Henry's oration (notwith-
standing William Wirt Henry's biography in the late nineteenth
century, in which he provided additional, but dubious,
testimony) is that he gave a speech and that several phrases did
linger in the minds of several hearers.

The subsequent fame of Henry's speech raises a question:
Why did so very few of the persons present who left records
even mention it? The reason may be that so much oratory at a
high pitch—little of it germane to the question—smothered the
impact of any single speech.

Thomas Marshall, however, was dazed by Henry's speech.
Standing outside by a church window, Edward Carrington
(many years later a mayor of Richmond) was so moved, it is
alleged, that he exclaimed that he wished to be buried on the
very spot where he stood, a wish supposedly honored at his
death in 1813.

The convention narrowly passed Henry's resolutions and appointed a defense committee with him at its head. Virginians
were not to regret the convention's action. In short order they
learned that the House of Lords had already voted down a proposal to withdraw troops from Boston. A bill in Parliament for
repeal of the Coercive Acts had failed, and the king had ad-
dressed the House of Commons, declaring the colonies in rebellion. Within a month there would be the clash at Lexington
and Concord and Lord Dunmore's seizure of the gunpowder at
Williamsburg; in three months, Bunker Hill. The decision to
take up arms came none too soon.

At the session on Friday, the first order of business was to
consider the report of the defense committee. Less than a day
after being appointed, the committee had ready a detailed
report updating the expired militia laws. Clearly several

members had come to the convention with definite ideas on the subject—Washington, Stephen, Lewis, and Henry. The delegates decided to postpone consideration of the committee's report until the next day.

Proceeding with the day's agenda, the convention discussed the New York legislature's refusal to elect delegates to the impending second Continental Congress. It also considered the report that New York had deserted the Continental Association, resolving "that a defection from such their compact would be a perfidy too atrocious to be charged on a sister Colony." The Virginia Committee of Correspondence should find out whether the report was true, and, if so, whether it could be regarded as binding on the people of New York.

In other business of the day the convention entreated Virginians to make contributions "for supplying the necessities and alleviating the distresses of our brave and worthy fellow-subjects of *Boston,* now suffering in the common cause of American freedom."

Saturday, the convention took up three major items; the courts, the militia system, and election of a seven-man delegation to Congress.

Since the dissolution of the Assembly in 1774, the act for the collection of fees by officers of the courts had expired. Some county courts, such as Chesterfield, declared that no fees could be collected until a new law was passed. The General Court, the highest court in the colony, ceased to function. Justices in the colony, however, did agree to try criminal cases and to do what was necessary to maintain law and order. The convention decided not to interfere with the existing void in the administration of justice.

The convention next discussed and adopted the committee's report on "the plan for embodying, arming, and disciplining the Militia." The plan proposed that each county have its militia "in constant training and readiness to act on any emergency," and, in addition, would form one or more volunteer companies of infantry and cavalry. A "Troop of Horse" was to consist of thirty rank and file, with appropriate officers, arms, and accoutrements. Uniforms were simply to be hunting shirts.

As dusk neared on the twenty-fifth, the delegates prepared to elect their representatives to Congress. Each member wrote seven names on a slip of paper and placed it in a ballot box. Peyton Randolph received the most votes, with 107; Washington, 106; Patrick Henry, 105. Richard Henry Lee, Edmund Pendleton, Benjamin Harrison, and Richard Bland were also elected. The convention then adjourned for the Sabbath, scheduling completion of its business for Monday.

On the final day, the convention approved a series of resolutions to establish economic self-sufficiency in the colony. With the main business completed, the delegates then wrapped up the session. They named Jefferson an alternate congressional delegate for Peyton Randolph, voted appreciation to Reverend Selden "for performing Divine Service," and "to the Town of *Richmond* and the neighbourhood, for their polite reception and entertainment of the Delegates."

Adjourning on Monday, March 27, the convention recommended to "the People of this Colony" that they choose delegates as soon as possible "to represent them in Convention for one year." It had been a hectic week. The delegates filed out of St. John's Church to return home, reflecting on what had been done, but little knowing that the storm was soon to begin.

County committees quickly met and approved the proceedings of the convention. So did the House of Burgesses, which finally reconvened in June. The House even sent "a faithful account of the Proceedings . . . and the reasons for the Resolutions" to Governor Dunmore.

Although it appeared that matters might calm down, an episode occurred on April 20 that aroused the emotions of Virginians and led to a show of armed resistance. The gunpowder affair is a familiar event in Virginia history and need not be retold here.

In Richmond, the inhabitants had been looking forward to the easing of tensions after the March convention. But the governor's seizure of the gunpowder, followed by his intractability and threats, provoked anger. Henricoans immediately formed an independent company in response to the crisis; hitherto they had dragged their feet in complying with the convention's defense resolutions.

The county committee of Henrico met in Richmond and resolved that the removal of the gunpowder "is an insult to every freeman in this County." Considering the act itself to be "a determined step, tending towards establishing that tyranny we so much dread," the committee resolved that every effort should be made to get immediate restitution of the powder. The local committee of correspondence was instructed to write its counterpart in Williamsburg, James City County, or York County for intelligence.

Richmonders looked forward to the reconvening of the Virginia Convention. Events were now taking place that would force the convention, like the Continental Congress itself, to move from preparing for war to conducting it. The third convention, like the March convention in Richmond and the one before in Williamsburg, would be an extralegal and extra-constitutional means of the community to secure specific objectives. Importantly, the resort to the convention form under-scored the principle that democratic government rests upon the continuing will of the people.

Because the governor had withdrawn from Williamsburg early in June and the Assembly could not legally function without him, Virginians had to settle for a *de facto* government. Thus the Richmond convention would have to act as both legislature and executive branch.

When the convention met at St. John's on July 17, most of the same delegates were back. George Mason, however, replaced George Washington. Thomas Jefferson was serving as an alternate for Peyton Randolph in congress. Randolph had returned for the House of Burgesses session and stayed in Virginia to act once again as president of the convention. Richard Bland attended, but other congressmen who were delegates to the convention—Patrick Henry, Richard Henry Lee, Benjamin Harrison, and Edmund Pendleton—remained in Philadelphia until Congress adjourned in early August before returning to the convention.

Up-country delegates joined with a solid bloc of German members from the Shenandoah Valley and such tidewater radicals as George Mason to make a slight majority. They favored having the convention assume full governmental powers and putting the armed forces in readiness for offensive action. What had provoked divided counsels at the March convention—raising militia volunteers—now was viewed with unanimity. Yet, for three weeks the convention was paralyzed by confusion.

The most heated issue centered on the radicals' proposal for an immediate standing army on regular pay. As George Mason put it: "During the first Part of the Convention Partys ran so high, that we had frequently no other Way of preventing improper Measures but by Procrastination, urging the previous Question, & giving Men time to reflect: however after some Weeks, the Bablers were pretty well silenced, a few weighty Members began to take the Lead. . . ."

The return of the congressional delegation on August 9 would strengthen the leadership at the convention. Actually, mutual trust lay beneath the surface factionalism, as was shown by the absence of power-play attempts to place any restrictions on candidacy, elections, or passing of resolutions.

The major topics for discussion included Indian affairs, raising a military force, frontier defense, and petitions from the counties on militia problems.

While the convention was considering military organization and was naming the commanding officers, groups of men, picturesque in their hunting shirts and rawhide leggings were marching daily to Williamsburg and Richmond. Recruits coming into Williamsburg were assured by the *Virginia Gazette* on July 28 that they would "be kindly received," would "enter into present pay and good quarters," and would be allowed a certain sum in advance to drink "Success to the liberties of America, and a happy issue out of all our troubles."

At the end of its third week, the convention elected a new seven-man congressional delegation. From a slate of twenty, Peyton Randolph again led the balloting; also elected were Richard Henry Lee, Thomas Jefferson, Benjamin Harrison, Thomas Nelson, Richard Bland, and George Wythe. Bland declined, and several days later Francis Lightfoot Lee was elected in his place.

In the final week, the convention approved seven ordinances. It had debated thoroughly those on raising military force (from which, in the final reading, the articles of war were made a separate enactment) and on arms and ammunition. The others had received little debate. Briefly, the ordinances passed by the third Virginia Convention in Richmond concerned: (1) raising a sufficient force for the defense of the colony; (2) oaths of officers and articles of war to govern the forces; (3) appointing a committee of safety to serve as supreme military council, accountable only to the next convention; (4) election of delegates and setting their meeting times and allowances, and also election of committeemen in the several counties; (5) appointing commissioners to settle the accounts of the militia and to make provision to pay the expense of raising the defense forces; (6) providing arms and ammunition for the use of the colony; and (7) paying the expenses of the delegates from Virginia to the General Congress.

With its monumental work accomplished, the convention selected Richmond as the site of a future fourth convention. It also voted on the last day, before adjourning, *A Declaration of the Delegates . . . setting forth the cause of their meeting, and the necessity of immediately putting the Country into a posture of defence, for the better protection of their lives, liberties, and properties.*

The declaration listed the grievances of Virginians: chiefly, the interference with legislative right, the removal of the powder, the governor's withdrawal from the seat of government, his solicitation for "Troops to be sent among us," and his "connivance at the detention of some of our slaves." It also cited "the remorseless fury with which General Gage and his coadjutors are endeavouring to spread fire, famine, and the most horrid desolation, throughout a sister Colony; of their insidious and cruel attempts to stir up the barbarous savages. . . ."

Virginians, the declaration asserted, would make every effort to restore peace and they would maintain their loyalty to the king, but not at the price of "our lives and properties, and . . . our just rights and privileges."

The convention had stopped just short of independence. It did not know that, three days before its adjournment, the king had declared the colonies in rebellion. A flicker of hope lingered that Great Britain would retract its coercive policies and would even concede the sole right of Americans to tax themselves. To the patriot view, there could be no other solution. Thomas Everard, writing to a merchant correspondent in London on the eve of the breakup of the convention, expressed an opinion of many Virginians:

Nothing can give all Americans more real Pleasure than a Reconciliation with Great Britain but rather than submit to an illegal and unjust Claim of Taxation the whole Continent are determined to defend their Rights to the last extremity. I hope the true friends to both Countries on your side the water will interpose and prevent the shedding of more blood in this Unnatural and unhappy dispute.

In accordance with the election ordinance of the convention, the freeholders of Henrico County met on Monday, November 6, to elect the county committee of safety. Reverend Miles Selden, Jr., was appointed chairman, and John Beckley, clerk. With fifteen of the twenty-one members sitting down to work, their chief business was to repass a resolution of the old committee that "no Provision, Fuel, or Naval Stores, be allowed to be waterborne, from this County, without the permission of the honourable Committee of Safety first had and obtained for that purpose."

Meanwhile, the colony-wide committee of safety had taken charge of the executive affairs of the colony. Unfortunately, the committee's records for the period to June 1776 have been lost. It met regularly at Williamsburg, but on two occasions it sat in the Richmond area. A brief meeting of several days took place at the end of the Richmond convention in August 1775. At some time, probably coinciding with the December 1 opening of the fourth convention, it met for several days in Richmond. The only evidence of such a meeting is an expense item for firewood to heat a room used by the committee in Richmond.

The fourth Virginia Convention assembled at St. John's Church on Friday, December 1, and promptly adjourned to reassemble at Williamsburg, which was still the capital. There Virginians did create an independent government four days before Congress voted the Declaration of Independence in Philadelphia. On June 29 in Williamsburg, the fifth Virginia Convention adopted a state constitution and elected Patrick Henry as governor (see fig. 13) and John Page as lieutenant governor. Henry was sick in bed, so Page ordered the printers of the two *Virginia Gazette*s to publish the Declaration and the sheriff of each county to announce it "at the Door of the Courthouse the first Court day after he shall receive the Same."

On the next court day in Richmond, which was August 5, the sheriff of Henrico County proclaimed the Declaration of Independence. The *Virginia Gazette* of Messrs. Dixon and Hunter in Williamsburg described the event as follows:

On Monday last, being Court day, the Declaration of Independence was publicly proclaimed to the town of Richmond, before a large concourse of respectable freeholders of Henrico County, and upwards of 200 militia, assembled on that great occasion. It was received with the universal shouts of joy, and re-echoed by three volleys of small arms. The same evening the town was illuminated, and the members of the committee held a club, where many patriotic toasts were drunk. Although there were near 1,000 people present, the whole was conducted with the utmost decorum, and the satisfaction visible on every countenance officially evidences their determination to support it with their lives and fortunes.

CHAPTER THREE

Richmond Becomes the Capital

IN EARLY 1779 Richmonders thought they would never get a firsthand taste of the war. Three years had passed since Dunmore's depredations at Norfolk. Only west of the mountains had there been occasional encounters with tories and Indians. Although enthusiasm and anxiety appeared to wane, Virginians, over the years, maintained a sizable contribution in men and supplies to Washington's army in the North.

A conquest of Virginia had undeniable military value to the British, and the year 1779 was to be a prologue to their invasion of the South. A British force from Florida took and held Augusta. Americans, however, successfully resisted attacks in South Carolina.

In May a British fleet under Vice Adm. Sir George Collier appeared in the lower Chesapeake, carrying an expeditionary force of 1,800 men commanded by Maj. Gen. Edward Matthews. These soldiers plundered and burned Portsmouth and Suffolk, the surrounding towns, and neighboring plantations. They destroyed a shipyard, a ropewalk, and naval stores, and seized 130 vessels and 3,000 hogsheads of tobacco. These "various Barbarities" caused the local militia to turn out "with alacrity." But by the time they were effectively in the field, the British had gone.

The Collier-Matthews raid had a clear secondary effect, however. It strengthened the hands of those up-country members of the House of Burgesses who wanted to move the capital to a safer place. As Virginia's frontier had moved westward, the center of population also shifted ever farther from the capital at Williamsburg. Western spokesmen from time to time expressed the opinion that the capital should be more centrally located.

That sentiment came out strongly when a fire gutted the capitol building at Williamsburg in 1746. Citizens of Goochland County sent two petitions to the Assembly in 1749 asking that the capital be moved to the falls of the James, where inland dwellers could reach it more easily. Again in 1772 the House of Burgesses passed a bill for the removal of the capital to Richmond, but the Council of State voted it down.

Thomas Jefferson's attempt in the fall of 1776 to have the capital moved to Richmond also failed. However, the state records were transferred to Richmond for safekeeping in the spring of 1777, as a result of a resolution by the General Assembly. Miles Selden, Jr., appointed keeper of the public records, rented a house in Richmond in which to store them.

Finally, on June 12, 1779, the General Assembly voted to move the capital. The legislators cited three main reasons: first, the capital should be as centrally located as possible; second, it should be on a navigable stream in order for the town that housed it to grow into an adequate state capital; third, and the immediate problem, it should not be "exposed to the insults and injuries of the publick enemy. . . ."

The Assembly agreed that these dangers "may be avoided and equal justice done to all the citizens of this commonwealth by removing the seat of government to the town of Richmond, in the county of Henrico, which is more safe and central than any other town situated on navigable water. . . ." The vote was close, however. According to one account, Richmond won by a single vote over a town in Hanover County.

The law that established Richmond as the new capital also made sweeping provisions for setting up the new seat of government. Six squares "on an open and airy part" of Richmond were to be appropriated for public buildings. The capitol, which was to house the General Assembly, was to be built on one of these squares. It would contain two chambers, one for the use of the House of Delegates and another for the Senate, as well as a lobby and rooms for conferences and committees.

On a second square, the Hall of Justice was to be built to provide space for the court of appeals, the high court of chancery, the court of admiralty, and the grand and petit juries. A public jail was to be built on the same lot.

One square was to be reserved for erecting at some future time a building to house executive boards and offices; two squares for the use of the governor; and the sixth square for a public market. The legislature prescribed that the above buildings be built "in a handsome manner with walls of brick or stone, and porticoes where the same may be convenient or ornamental, and with pillars and pavements of stone."

To oversee the acquisition of property and the erection of the public buildings, both houses of the Assembly were to elect five persons to be designated the Directors of Public Buildings. Strict rules governed the acquisition of the property. When the directors had chosen the land, the sheriff of Henrico County was to call twelve freeholders to meet at the property and appraise its value. The freeholders were to have no interest in the lots and could not be related to the owners or proprietors. From the time they arrived at the property until the final decision was sealed and turned over to the sheriff the freeholders were to take nothing "either of meat or drink from any person."

These elaborate plans could not be carried out immediately. Because of the war, prices were high and building materials and labor scarce. The first permanent public building would not be erected for another six years. Instead, the General Assembly instructed the Directors of Public Buildings to build or otherwise provide temporary buildings for the use of the government "with all convenient speed."

The Henrico County jail was to be enlarged for use as the public jail. Facilities to house the courts and the General Assembly were to be available by the end of April 1780, after which date the courts and the Assembly would meet in Richmond. The Directors of Public Buildings were to spend no more than £20,000 in providing these temporary buildings. Any action toward acquiring property for the permanent buildings was delayed indefinitely.

On June 24, 1779, the General Assembly appointed Turner Southall and James Buchanan of Richmond, Archibald Cary and Robert Goode of Chesterfield County, and Robert Carter Nicholas of Hanover County as Directors of Public Buildings for Richmond. They immediately began taking steps to provide the necessary temporary public buildings. As one of their first actions, they asked Governor Thomas Jefferson to supply locks, hinges, glass, and nails.

In July the directors placed the following ad in the *Virginia*

Gazette, published at Williamsburg:

The directors appointed by the General Assembly to provide temporary buildings for the two Houses of Assembly, the Courts of Justice, several publick Boards, and a publick jail, give notice that they will meet at Mr. *Hogg's* tavern, in the town of *Richmond,* the day after *Henrico* Court, in next month, to agree with workmen for undertaking the said buildings. Bond with approved security will be required for the performance; one half of the money to be paid within one month of the time the work is let, the other when it is finished. A plan of the buildings shall be lodged in the hands of Mr. *Hogg* and of Mr. *Galt* in the said town, a week before.

By November the directors reported that they had let buildings, which were to be finished in April 1780.

Although the above advertisement suggests that the directors built new buildings of a temporary nature, reason argues to the contrary. Buildings confiscated from British companies and loyalist Americans stood vacant and immediately available. The Assembly and various departments of government actually used some of them; other departments occupied rented quarters.

Convincing evidence that the directors made repairs and changes in older buildings rather than constructing new ones appears in the report of a House committee to investigate the directors' accounts. The directors had paid a total of £21,198 8s. 11d. for labor and materials put into repairs and alterations. That amount slightly exceeded the £20,000 maximum allocated for temporary buildings—with no mention of outlays for *new* buildings.

The actual moving of the capital from Williamsburg to Richmond took place in April 1780. Archibald Blair, clerk of the Council, put a notice in the March 25, 1780, *Virginia Gazette* that: "the business of government, in the executive department will cease to be transacted at Williamsburg from the 7th of April next, and will commence at Richmond, on the 24th of the same month. The Governour will be in *Richmond* during the interval, to do such business as may be done by him, without the concurrence of the publick boards."

Jefferson instructed the Board of Trade to have one or more vessels at the nearest landing on the evening of April 7 "to receive & convey to Richmond the presses, books, papers, & implements of the offices of council, War, Trade, Auditors, & Register and furniture of the Capitol & Palace." An armed vessel furnished by the Board of War was to "receive the treasury with its implements" and escort the other ships.

Though the Directors of Public Buildings had provided temporary buildings for the use of the General Assembly, the courts of justice, and several public boards, Richmond was such a small town that some employees of the government had difficulty finding adequate accommodations for themselves and their work. The commonwealth printers, Clarkson and Davis, petitioned the House of Delegates on May 12, 1780, for more time to move to Richmond, as they had not been able to find a house where they could carry out their work as public printers.

In describing her family's move to Richmond from York, by way of Williamsburg, Betsy Ambler, daughter of State Treasurer Jacquelin Ambler and future sister-in-law of John Marshall (see fig. 11) gave this interesting observation of the housing situation in Richmond:

Nothing material happened on our way, and we arrived on the evening of the second day at this famous Metropolis; for so we may now call it, as all heads of departments, like ourselves, have arrived here in safety. But where we are to lay our weary heads Heaven knows; so recently has it become a place of any consequence that accommodations cannot be found for one half the people who are necessarily brought here. It is indeed a lovely situation, and may at some future period be a great city, but at present it will scarce afford one comfort in life.

With the exception of two or three families this little town is made up of Scotch factors, who inhabit small tenements scattered here and there from the river to the hill. Some of them look, as Colonel Marshall observed, as if the poor Caledonians had brought them over on their backs, the weakest of them being glad enough to stop at the bottom of the hill, others a little stronger proceeding higher, whilst a few of the stoutest and the boldest reached the summit.

One of these hardy Scots has thought proper to vacate his little dwelling on the hill, and though our whole family can scarcely stand up all together in it, my father has determined to rent it as the only decent tenement on the hill.

The Directors of Public Buildings had hoped that economic incentive would stimulate private individuals to help solve the problem of housing by building accommodations close to the capitol. But little had been done. Not until its first session in Richmond, starting May 1, 1780, did the General Assembly pass an act to end the uncertainty over exactly where in Richmond the capitol would be located.

The Assembly decided that the "capitol, halls of justice, state house for the executive boards, and an house for the governour" would be located on Shockoe Hill. The public market was to be established immediately and located below Shockoe Hill on the west side of Shockoe Creek.

In the same act, the General Assembly appointed additional Directors of Public Buildings and expanded their assignments. In addition to Cary, Nicholas, Southall, Goode, and Buchanan, the Assembly appointed Thomas Jefferson, Richard Adams, Edmund Randolph, and Samuel DuVal as directors.

Among their new duties was that of laying out in squares the remainder of Richmond. These new streets and all the streets on Shockoe Hill were to be at least 80 feet wide and not more than 120 feet wide. Any house already in existence that would block the new streets, or other streets already in existence, would be allowed to stand twenty years but must then be removed. To deal with the problem of travel up and down the hills in Richmond, the directors were to lay out streets "straight or curved," as would most facilitate travel.

On July 17, 1780, seven of the directors met and named the streets of Richmond. They designated by letters the streets running east and west, with the street in the western part of the town nearest the water being assigned the letter A. Each succeeding street north would receive the next letter. What is today Cary Street then became D Street, Main Street being E Street, Franklin Street being F Street, Grace Street, G Street, and Broad Street, H Street. The cross streets running north and south were designated by numbers—starting with First Street as the westernmost street of the town, with numbers increasing to the east. The streets so numbered still retain their original designations.

The choice of Shockoe Hill as the location for the capitol had an interesting personal dimension involving one of the Directors of Public Buildings, prominent Richmond citizen Richard Adams. Adams, who served as a member of the House of Delegates and was senator from Henrico, Louisa, and Goochland counties from 1778 to 1782, owned most of the part of Richmond known today as Church Hill, then called Richmond Hill. According to Eliza Griffin Carrington, his granddaughter, Adams was a close friend of Thomas Jefferson's and often entertained him in his home on Richmond Hill. On one of these occasions, shortly before the resolution was passed to move the capital to Richmond, Jefferson pledged, if the capital was moved, to secure the location of the public buildings on Richmond Hill. For his part, Adams promised to donate the sites for the government buildings. After Shockoe Hill was chosen for the site of the public buildings, Adams never forgave Jefferson.

Even after the Assembly decided that Shockoe Hill would be the site of the permanent capitol, Adams apparently continued to agitate. As late as June 1783 rumors persisted that the site would be Richmond Hill instead of Shockoe Hill. The uncertainty retarded growth of the city on Shockoe Hill.

In an effort to make a final determination, the House of Delegates appointed a committee to consult with the Directors of Public Buildings. Richard Adams appeared before the committee as one of the two owners of lots on Richmond Hill, and Horatio Turpin as owner of the most valuable lots suited to government use on Shockoe Hill. Adams offered to donate twelve lots on Richmond Hill for the use of the state, while Turpin would give five lots, or two and one-half acres, to the public on Shockoe Hill if the commonwealth would purchase the buildings on them.

The committee recommended "That the present and future holders of lots on Shockoe hill be assured that it is the determination of the General Assembly to continue the preference hitherto given to Shockoe hill, as the situation of the public buildings . . ."

The recommendation to use Shockoe for the capital buildings was put to the House in the form of a resolution. But at this point dissatisfaction with the capital's being anywhere in Richmond surfaced. An amendment was offered that "the seat of government ought to be removed from the city of Richmond to the city of Williamsburg." Some government officials had disliked the move from the beginning. David Jameson, a member of the Council of State, wrote to James Madison shortly after the capital was moved to Richmond.

Richmond must one day or other be a great Town and were we in Peace I should think it a proper place for the Seat of Government. at present I do not think it so I believe I shall never be reconciled to it as a desirable place of residence. half the mornings since I have been here the Town has been covered with Fog. if so at this Season, what may we not dread in August? and who not used to it, can stand the thin putrid state of the Air? I have been long used to the Salt Air and think I cannot enjoy health without it.

Although thirty-nine delegates favored the return to Williamsburg, fifty-five voted against the amendment and so defeated it. The House then reaffirmed its preference for Shockoe Hill as the location of the government buildings.

The Directors of Public Buildings could now continue with condemnation proceedings to obtain six squares for public buildings on Shockoe Hill, which would be known as Capitol Square. These proceedings had started in April 1781 and were completed August 17, 1784. Twelve-man juries summoned by the sheriff of Henrico County assigned a value to the lots being taken. Owners of some of the lots were not known.

In the meantime, before a permanent capitol rose on Shockoe Hill, the Assembly met at the bottom of the hill in what had been the William Cuninghame and Company property, confiscated by the state March 6, 1780. This property consisted of four lots including a dwelling house, storehouse, warehouse, and other structures.

The main building, used by the House of Delegates, stood on the northwest corner of Cary and Fourteenth streets. Dr. Schoepf wrote of it: "The Assembly had just now come together for its yearly winter session; a small frame building serves the purpose, used also on occasion, with change of scene, for balls and public banquets." Samuel Mordecai, who saw the "Old Capitol" in the early 1800s, described it as "a plain one-story building, originally of small dimensions."

The Senate seems to have met in an adjacent building, later known as the Old Senate House.

The General Assembly held sessions in Richmond each spring and each fall, beginning in May 1780. The Hessian doctor, seeing the Virginians through his European prejudices, gave the following account of the Assembly in 1783.

It is said of the Assembly: It sits; but this is not a just expression, for these members show themselves in every possible position rather than that of sitting still, with dignity and attention. An assembly of men whose object is the serious and important one of making laws, should at least observe a certain decorum, but independence prevails even here. During the visits I made I saw this estimable assembly quiet not 5 minutes together; some are leaving, others coming in, most of them talking of insignificant or irrelevant matters, and to judge from the indifference and heedlessness of most of their faces it must be a trifling business to make laws. At the open door of the hall stands a doorkeeper, who is almost incessantly and with a loud voice calling out for one member after another. In the ante-room there is a tumult quite as constant, here they amuse themselves zealously with talk of horseraces, runaway negroes, yesterday's play, politics, or it may be, with trafficking.

Nor did he feel the dress of the legislators was fitting for the occasion: "In the same clothes in which one goes hunting or tends his tobacco-fields, it is permissable to appear in the Senate or the Assembly. There are displayed boots, trowsers, stockings, and Indian leggings; great-coats, ordinary coats, and short jackets, according to each man's caprice or comfort, and all equally honorable." Schoepf commented on the actual workings in the General Assembly:

As in all other public and private societies there are certain men who lead the debate, and think and speak for the rest, so it is also in these Assemblies. Among the orators here is a certain Mr. Henry who appears to have the greatest influence over the House. He has a high-flown and bold delivery, deals more in words than in reasons, and not so long ago was a country schoolmaster. Men of this stamp, either naturally eloquent or become so through their occupation, as e.g. lawyers, invariably take the most active and influential part in these Assemblies; the other members, for the most part farmers without clear and refined ideas, with little education or knowledge of the world, are merely there to give their votes, which are sought, whenever the House is divided into parties, by the insinuations of agreeable manners and in other ways.

When the opinion of the House is to be taken regarding a question in debate, the Speaker calls first for the *Ayes* and then the *Noes*, given

Fig. 12. Archibald Cary. Cary, who
lived just below Richmond at
Ampthill, was speaker of the Virginia
Senate, and was prominent in Richmond life during the Revolution.
This painting is by Anne Fletcher
from the original picture that hung
in the Governor's Mansion and was
destroyed by fire in 1926. (Courtesy
of the Virginia State Library.)

together in a loud voice by all the members present, and with a critical
ear the Speaker judges from the strength of the noise whether the
affirmative or the negative votes are in a majority. But if the votes are
so distributed that the ear cannot plainly distinguish them, a "division" of the House is demanded, and the members form themselves
into two groups and are counted.

   Schoepf echoed the opinion of Archibald Cary (see fig. 12) of
Chesterfield County, who served as speaker of the Senate from
1776 through 1783, except for one session in 1779 when he was
ill. During his illness, just before the Assembly moved to Richmond, Cary wrote to Jefferson criticizing the General
Assembly. He pointed out that the body was beginning to be

held in low esteem because of its own misconduct, such as drinking and gambling, which was employing the members not only at night but through the day as well.

From the time the capital was moved to Richmond in 1780 until the end of the Revolution in 1783, the state had three governors and one acting governor. Thomas Jefferson, elected governor in June 1779, served for two years (see fig. 14). Stepping down June 3, 1781, he refused to run for reelection because he felt the commonwealth needed a governor with military experience.

When Governor Jefferson arrived in Richmond in April of 1780, he rented a house for one year from Thomas Turpin, Sr., husband of his aunt, Mary Jefferson. Speaking of this governor's mansion, Jefferson's slave Isaac described it as a "wooden house near where the palace stands now." According to Isaac, the house and grounds included a wine cellar, a corn-crib, and a meat house.

Jefferson agreed to 8,000 pounds of tobacco for the year's rent, though he thought it high. He realized, however, that the price was in line with rent increases in Richmond since the capital had moved there. In September 1782 the commonwealth agreed to pay this rent to Turpin.

Though never proved conclusively, the most likely location of Jefferson's residence in Richmond was on Turpin's lot no. 367 on Shockoe Hill. This would be south of the present governor's residence, where Twelfth Street and Franklin Street would meet if they continued through the present Capitol Square grounds.

Thomas Nelson, Jr., of Yorktown (see fig. 15) served as governor from June 12 to November 30, 1781. Nelson's Richmond residence has not been determined. Governor Nelson was in the field most of his six-month term and probably did not occupy an official residence in Richmond. However, he may have lived in the same house that his successor, Governor Harrison, occupied.

Benjamin Harrison (see fig. 16) became governor December 1, 1781, and served in that position for three one-year terms. Exactly where Governor Harrison lived during his years in office has been a matter of debate. The official records, however, contain clear and specific evidence that a "tenement

Fig. 13 Patrick Henry. Served as first governor of Virginia during the American Revolution, 1776–79, while the capital was still Williamsburg. (Courtesy of the Virginia State Library.)

Fig. 14. Thomas Jefferson. The second Virginia governor during the revolutionary war, 1779–81, Jefferson was the first governor to serve in Richmond as the capital. (Courtesy of the Virginia State Library.)

Fig. 15. Thomas Nelson. Third governor of Virginia, he served in 1781. (Courtesy of the Virginia State Library.)

Fig. 16. Benjamin Harrison. Fourth governor of Virginia, he served during 1781–84. (Courtesy of the Virginia State Library.)

and four lots," at first rented, then purchased by the government from James Marsden, were occupied by Governor Harrison throughout his three terms. The house, which became known as the old "Palace," served succeeding governors until work began on a new governor's mansion in 1811.

The marquis de Chastellux, who visited Governor Harrison in April 1782, described the governor's residence as "a homely, but spacious enough house, which was fitted up for him." Mordecai remembered it as "a very plain wooden building of two stories, with only two moderate-sized rooms on the first floor."

Marsden's four lots were nos. 358, 368, 369, and 380, all in the area of the present governor's mansion and near the house Jefferson rented from Turpin. The most likely lot for the residence was 358, which places Harrison's residence on the present Capitol Square Grounds, just slightly to the south and east of the present governor's mansion and directly east of the present state capitol.

During Harrison's administration, the Council of State used for its meetings a brick house, also owned by Colonel Turpin, on the hill behind the governor's residence. The summit of the hill (dug away preceding the Civil War) thus acquired the name of Council Chamber Hill.

After the capital was moved to Richmond, a Richmond lodge of the Masons was chartered December 28, 1780. Prominent Richmonders who were members included Edmund Randolph, Samuel Scherer, John Marshall, David Lambert, John Beckley, and Gabriel Galt. Galt either gave or sold to the Masons land on which they built a Masonic Hall in 1787. The hall, reported to be the first building erected especially for Masonic meetings in America, still stands on Franklin Street, between Eighteenth and Nineteenth streets.

No institution was more important in the social life of early Richmond than its taverns—also called inns or ordinaries, with the three terms used interchangeably. Men of the community gathered to eat or drink, to politick, to gossip, to play billiards, and to hear the latest news from travelers. After the capital was moved to Richmond, the local taverns increased in importance, providing board for members of the General Assembly and for other people who had business with the state. The Henrico County Court and the Richmond hustings court licensed fifteen men and one woman to keep taverns in Richmond during the years 1781, 1782, and 1783.

Serafino Formicola, a Neapolitan by birth, operated a tavern popular in Richmond during the Revolution. It stood on the south side of Main Street, west of Shockoe Creek between Fifteenth and Seventeenth streets. Schoepf described the tavern and its patrons thus:

The entire house contained but two large rooms on the ground-floor, and two of the same size above, the apartments under the roof furnished with numerous beds standing close together, both rooms and chambers standing open to every person throughout the day. Here, no less than in most of the other public-houses in America, it is expected that rooms are to be used only as places for sleeping, eating and drinking. The whole day long, therefore, one is compelled to be among all sorts of company and at night to sleep in like manner; thus travellers, almost anywhere in America, must renounce the pleasure of withdrawing apart, (for their own convenience or their own affairs), from the noisy, disturbing, or curious crowd, unless it may be, that staying at one place for some time, a private apartment is to be rented. The Assembly meeting at this time was the occasion of a great gathering of strangers and guests at Richmond, and every evening our inn was very full. Generals, Colonels, Captains, Senators, Assemblymen, Judges, Doctors, Clerks, and crowds of Gentlemen, of every weight and calibre and every hue of dress, sat all together about the fire, drinking, smoking, singing, and talking ribaldry. There is in this no great ground of complaint, because such a company at other times may be very agreeable, entertaining, and instructive; but the indelicate custom of having so many beds together in one room is the more surprising, since elsewhere in America there is much store set by decorum and neatness, which by such an arrangement as this must often be dispensed with.

Another major tavern, Gabriel Galt's, stood on the northwest corner of Main and Nineteenth streets. Galt's Tavern, referred to in later years as City Tavern, opened in 1775 and reported among its customers respectively, Arnold, Simcoe, Cornwallis and Lafayette, who made the tavern their headquarters. The Continental officer Feltman described in his journal playing billiards at Galt's Tavern and dining "very sumptuously upon Rock fish." On one occasion Feltman and a companion reported playing billiards all night. Galt's Tavern was also the most popular place in Richmond for auctions.

One of the oldest taverns in town belonged to Abraham Cowley, who received his original license in 1737. His tavern occupied the southwest corner of Main and Twenty-third streets, near the county courthouse. In 1776 Cowley advertised his ordinary for rent, and described it as follows: ". . . the house is large, very commodious, a good kitchen, dairy, meethouse, new stable, that will contain 74 horses. . . ." Cowley also pointed out that, being convenient to the courthouse, it received the largest part of the business created by court days. During the war years the appropriately named Stephen Tankard operated this tavern.

Richard Hogg kept a popular tavern at the southwest corner of Main and Fifteenth streets, near Byrd's warehouses. Known as the Old Tavern, it was taken over in 1783 by Samuel Trower.

The ordinaries were tightly regulated by the county courts and subsequently by the Richmond hustings court. The court issued licenses to tavern keepers, and set all prices for "liquors, diet, lodging, provender, stablage, fodder, and pasturage. . . ." Within one month after they were established, a table of the rates was to be "openly set up in the publick entertaining room of every ordinary."

In April 1783 the hustings court decreed the following rates for Richmond taverns:

For a Breakfast or Supper	two shillings
For a Dinner	two shillings and six pence
For one night's lodging	one shilling
For a Servant's Diet	one shilling
For a quart of Madeira Wine	six shillings
For a Quart of port Wine	four shillings
For a quart of Rum Punch made with loaf sugar	two shillings and six pence
For a quart of Rum or Brandy Toddy	one shilling and six pence
For a jill of Rum or French Brandy	six pence
For a jill of common Brandy or Whiskey	four pence
For a Gallon of Corn or Oats	ten pence
For a pound of Hay or Fodder	two pence
For stablage or pasturage for one horse one night	seven pence half penney

The courts on occasion exercised their power to revoke a license. In August 1782 the Henrico County Court withdrew

William Almond's license to keep a tavern in Richmond, as he had been found to keep a "riotous and disorderly house." John Lockley, who had received a license to keep a tavern in his home at Rocketts landing in June 1783, was summoned before the hustings court meeting in August to answer charges that "he keeps a very disorderly House and entertains and retails Liquor to Negroes." Witnesses supported the charges, and Lockley lost his tavern license for one month.

Both men and women played billiards, backgammon, and other dice games, as well as such card games as whist and poker. All were played for money. The Richmond Common Hall outlawed the playing of any games on the Sabbath.

Lotteries were a popular form of gambling and an often used way of raising money. The city itself existed as a result of Byrd's lottery in which he disposed of city lots while raising money to better his own financial position. At one time the Common Hall set up a lottery to raise money to build a stone bridge over Shockoe Creek. The plan, never carried out, was to sell 4,000 tickets at seven dollars each. Of the 4,000 tickets, 1,335 would be prizes and 2,665 blanks, or almost two blanks to a prize.

A law passed by the General Assembly in 1779 voided previous gambling debts and outlawed gambling for sums larger than £5. Tavern keepers were not to allow gambling in their taverns. The law forebade individuals to raise money by the use of a lottery. A person who violated the law made himself ineligible to hold any office in the state for two years.

A group of freeholders in Chesterfield County condemned excessive gambling because "by too free and common an exercise [of] that pernicious practice, especially at public houses, idleness was encouraged, and the morals of youth in a great degree corrupted." But they felt that the act went too far. They cited the need for a "good and well appointed cavalry" and the economic desirability of encouraging the development of Virginia's breed of horses as grounds for allowing properly supervised horse racing.

That Chesterfield petition reflected the strong interest in riding and racing that had existed in the Richmond area for a long time. To almost every Virginian, *his* horse was the most prized possession, and one traveler told of people who would walk five miles to catch a horse in order to ride for one mile. Schoepf

Fig. 17. John Dixon. He was the publisher of the *Virginia Gazette,* which was moved to Richmond when it became the state capital in 1780. (Courtesy of the Valentine Museum, Richmond, Va.)

Fig. 18. Portrait of Rosanna Dixon and her daughter. Mrs. Dixon's husband was Richmond printer John Dixon. (Courtesy of the Valentine Museum, Richmond, Va.)

commented on the horses in Richmond when the Assembly met: "One could almost fancy it was an Arabian village; there were to be seen the whole day long saddled horses at every turn, and a swarming of riders in the few and muddy streets, for a horse must be mounted, if only to fetch a prise of snuff from across the way; but of coaches there were none, which in the larger towns elsewhere jolt through all the streets."

When the capital moved from Williamsburg, Richmond acquired its first newspaper. The printing establishment of John Dixon (see figs. 17 and 18) and Thomas Nicolson moved its *Virginia Gazette* after the Williamsburg edition of April 8, 1780. Dixon and Nicolson printed their paper in Richmond through May 19, 1781. They also printed such items for the state government as broadsides, acts passed by the General Assembly, journals of the House of Delegates, and journals of the Senate. The firm printed and sold *The Virginia Almanack for 1781,* and the one for 1782.

Probably Dixon and Nicolson could not adequately do the

state printing, or, less likely, their loyalty was suspect. At any rate, in 1780 the General Assembly authorized the governor, with the advice of the council, to engage "a good and able printer, of firm and known attachment to the independence of the United States, . . . to bring a good and well provided press into this commonwealth." The partnership of Dixon and Nicolson was dissolved in May 1781.

Governor Jefferson appointed John Dunlap and James Hayes the new public printers. Dunlap, a well-known Pennsylvania printer who had been appointed printer to Congress in 1778, probably did no more than provide financial backing. James Hayes actually ran the printing operation in Richmond. This partnership started a new newspaper, *The Virginia Gazette, or, the American Advertiser,* the first issue appearing December 22, 1781.

Dunlap and Hayes did all kinds of government printing, as had Dixon and Nicolson earlier. Like many others at the time, they experienced difficulty in collecting from the hard-pressed state treasury and petitioned the House of Delegates May 13, 1783, pointing out that, of £300 voted them by the last session as absolutely necessary for the immediate procurement of paper and other necessaries, they had received only £30. Because of their lack of funds, Dunlap and Hayes had been unable to purchase from Philadelphia materials needed to carry out the government printing. Hayes also served as postmaster.

After the partnership between Dixon and Nicolson dissolved, William Prentis and Thomas Nicolson entered a partnership and started publishing *The Virginia Gazette, and Weekly Advertiser* in Richmond in December 1781. Nicolson and Prentis also printed broadsides and the yearly almanacs.

John Dixon and John Hunter Holt—a former Norfolk printer recently returned from the army—joined together to publish *The Virginia Gazette or The Independent Chronicle,* the first issue of which appeared August 23, 1783. It brought to three the number of newspapers being published in Richmond in 1783, more than in most American cities today.

Thus, in many ways the transplantation of the capital to Richmond stimulated the town's growth and itself marked a milestone on Richmond's journey to becoming a major city. The marquis de Chastellux commented that:

Though Richmond be already an old town, and well situated for trade, being built on the spot where James river begins to be navigable, that is, just below the Rapids, it was, before the war, one of the least considerable in Virginia, where they are all, in general, very small; but the seat of government having been removed from Williamsburg, it is become a real capital, and is augmenting every day.

CHAPTER FOUR

Richmond Becomes a City

ALTHOUGH RICHMOND had been formally established as a town in 1752, it remained without a real government of its own. The town's trustees had very limited powers. For thirty years the only local government in Richmond was that of Henrico County.

Virginia's new constitution adopted the colonial system of county government almost unchanged. The key to that system was the county court, composed of justices of the peace appointed by the governor. They served for life and without pay, and they controlled all aspects of local government, exercising a mixture of executive and legislative authority in addition to their judicial authority.

When vacancies occurred among the justices of a county court, the remaining members nominated new members from among the county's wealthy and influential families; the people at large had no voice in choosing their county officials. The only elections held in Henrico County before 1782 were to elect delegates and senators to the General Assembly, and only male freeholders could vote in those elections. In an unincorporated town like Richmond, that meant only men who owned a house and at least part of a lot, or who leased a house for life. Males under twenty-one, women, free blacks, mulattoes, Indians, and slaves had no vote.

As the Henrico County Court records covering the revolutionary period before October 1781 were destroyed by the British, only the justices serving from that time forward are known. The list includes the names of prominent Richmonders: Turner Southall, Nathaniel Wilkinson, Miles Selden, Jr., Thomas Prosser, Isaac Younghusband, John Hales, Richard Adams, Samuel DuVal, John Pleasants, Bowler Cocke, Edmund Randolph, John Pendleton, Jr., Peyton Randolph, Daniel Lawrence Hylton, James Buchanan, and William Foushee.

The first nine of those same men also served as a special commission to take written testimony about deeds, wills, inventories, and other documents destroyed by the British. In that way the county hoped to reconstitute as accurately as possible its lost records.

The county court had the responsibility of recording deeds and wills and appraising estates. It heard cases involving personal disputes, assault and battery, and trespass. The greatest number of cases concerned debt.

The court investigated the emancipation of slaves and recorded deeds of emancipation. Orphans were the responsibility of the court, which appointed guardians for orphans left with an estate. Those without an estate were bound out as apprentices by the churchwardens of Henrico parish. The court also assumed the role of supplying provisions for families of soldiers killed in the war.

The Henrico County Court had a special duty in the area of health. During an outbreak of smallpox in February 1782, the court established a hospital—referred to as a pest house—for isolating people with the disease. Superintended by Commissioners James Buchanan, Gabriel Galt, Thomas Prosser, and Miles Selden, Jr., the pest house was located on the plantation of John Cocke in a house in the possession of William Foushee. Dr. Foushee could inoculate anyone who applied to him there. Some petitioned the court to have their inoculations at home.

A major responsibility of the county court was the provision and maintenance of county roads. The county had a number of road surveyors, each one responsible for a particular road or for a part of the county. The county paid for road materials and for timber for bridges. Creeks, declared to be public highways, were to be kept clear by the surveyor. Any surveyor found guilty by the grand jury of failing to do his job was subject to a fine of £10.

Grand juries summoned by Henrico County Court made numerous presentments against road surveyors for not keeping the roads in their charge in good repair. On November 5, 1781, the surveyor of the "three chopped road" (the main road leading west from Richmond) received a summons. Even the trustees of Richmond had to appear in court for failing to keep the streets in repair.

Seven months later the court took into its own hands the

problem of Richmond's streets. Justices Younghusband and
Selden were appointed to let a contract for the necessary
repairs to Main Street near John Clark's lot, with the county
bearing the expense.

Tobacco being vital to the economy of Virginia, the county
court exercised broad powers on behalf of the state in assuring
adequate warehouses. When a proprietor declined to enlarge
or rebuild his warehouse, the court ordered the work to be
done and to be paid for from warehouse fees. After James
Lyles refused to rebuild the Shockoe warehouses, destroyed by
the British in 1781, the court had Isaac Younghusband and
Turner Southall let the rebuilding to Drury Wood. The court
had an additional tobacco warehouse built at Shockoe in 1783.
Similar power was exercised against Charles Lewis, owner of
Rocketts warehouses.

The county court also acted for the state in the collection of
the tithe, or poll tax. This tax was levied on all males, including
slaves, over sixteen and on all female slaves over eighteen. The
owner paid the tax on his slaves. Persons subject to the tax were
called "tithables." In March 1782 the court divided Henrico
County into seven precincts, the seventh being Richmond.
Miles B. Selden, Jr., was appointed to take the list of tithables
and of all taxable property in the seventh precinct.

Money was so scarce in 1782 that the state began to accept tobacco, hemp, and flour in payment of taxes, making the county
responsible for its collection and safekeeping. Thomas Prosser
and John Pleasants became commissioners of the grain tax in
the county, and Prosser and Nathaniel Wilkinson were appointed "to provide good and sufficient Houses for the reception and safekeeping of Hemp and Flour" taken as taxes. In
March 1782 the court appointed Samuel Ege and Dabney
Miller "to receive, safely to keep and to deliver the Hemp and
Flour and also to inspect the said hemp, which may be delivered at the Public Inspection in the Town of Richmond as established by . . . Act of Assembly."

The government of the county included three positions
closely related to the county court: the sheriff, the clerk, and
the attorney for the commonwealth. Since Richmond had no
city government, all three functioned for the town as part of
the county. The Henrico County sheriff also served the

General Court of Virginia after the capital was moved to Richmond.

Richmond grew rapidly in population and importance after it became the state capital in the spring of 1780. But for two more years it remained a town without its own government. Finally, sixty-five citizens signed and sent to the General Assembly a petition (see fig. 19) dated May 28, 1782:

To the Honorable the Speaker and the Gentlemen of the House of Delegates, the Petition of the Inhabitants of the Town of Richmond Humbly sheweth That your Petitioners, actuated by a Love of Order & good Government, are desireous the Town of Richmond should be incorporated and therefore pray your honorable House that the same may be incorporated under the name of the City of Richmond & with jurisdiction to extend two miles all round the present extremities of the Town and under such other Establishment as may be most conducive to the Peace, Happiness, and good Government of the Inhabitants, . . .

The Assembly responded with an act incorporating the city of Richmond. Perhaps because Richmond was a mercantile city with a mobile populace, the legislature set liberal voter qualifications. An owner of a lot in the city could vote whether he lived in the city or not and whether the lot was improved or not. Persons who had lived in Richmond at least three months and possessed movable or immovable property worth 100 pounds could vote.

Eligible voters were to elect twelve "fit and able men," freeholders and inhabitants, to serve as a city government. These twelve, referred to as the Common Hall, would then publicly elect a mayor, a recorder, and four aldermen from among themselves. The other six men would be common councilmen.

An election for all twelve would take place every three years. Any of the twelve could be reelected; however, no person could serve as mayor for more than one year in any two-year period. A vacancy occurring before the end of the three-year term would be filled by the remainder of the Common Hall. Vacancies in the office of mayor or recorder were to be filled from the aldermen; in the office of alderman, from the common council; in the common council, from freeholders and in-

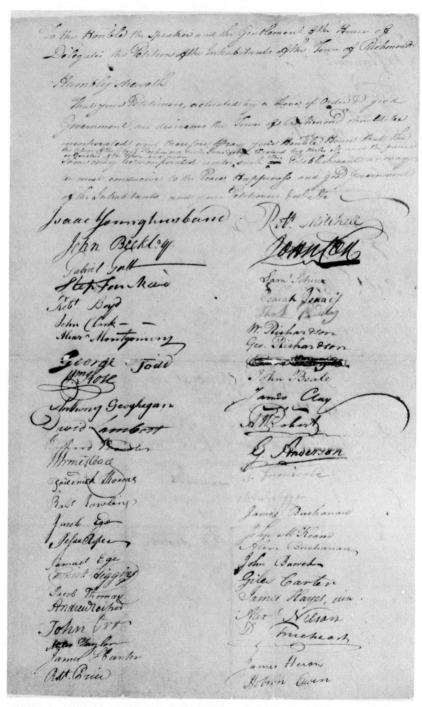

Fig. 19.   Petition from Richmond citizens to the state legislature. This petition was sent in 1782, requesting that Richmond be chartered as a city with its own government. (Courtesy of the Virginia State Library.)

habitants of the city. Ordinary-keepers could not hold office in the Common Hall.

The incorporating act defined the powers of the city of Richmond. The city had the right to acquire and dispose of property, to sue and be sued in court, and to make bylaws, rules, and ordinances necessary for the benefit of the people of the city—as long as they did not violate the state's constitution or laws.

Richmond could build and repair public buildings, purchase fire engines and hire firemen, have wells dug, and provide pumps for a water supply. The city could also provide "hospitals for the reception of persons infected with contagious disorders," and it could "pay the charge of removing such infected persons to the hospital" and provide "doctors, nurses and other necessary attendants, as well as guards to prevent the spreading of such disorders."

The city government had the power to repair the streets and to hire a watchman. The city could hold a fair each year on the first Thursday in May and another on the first Thursday in October. Disorderly persons who had not been resident of the city for twelve months could be expelled.

To effect all the above grants of power, the city was empowered to raise revenue through taxes. The city could tax all white and black male tithables and all property, both real and personal, in the city. Richmond could levy a duty on ships using wharves built by the city, to pay for these wharves and to keep them in repair. The city had the power to fix fees "upon every billiard-table and tippling house, booth or tent within the jurisdiction of the corporation," and "demand resonable fees for every ordinary license within the same, over and above those established for raising a revenue."

The mayor, the recorder, and the four aldermen also had judicial power within the city and for one mile around it on the north side of the James River. Any four or more of these officials were empowered to hold a court of hustings, with jurisdiction over minor cases originating within the city. They could also examine criminals for all offenses committed within the city.

The clerk, acting under the authority of the court, had the sole power of "licensing tavern-keepers and settling their rates, appointing a clerk of the market, establishing an assize of bread, wine, wood, coal, . . . and also appointing a sergeant, who shall have the power of a sheriff, constables, and other necessary officers of the court, and surveyors of the streets." The law allowed the officers of the court to collect the same fees as were allowed to the clerk and sheriff of Henrico County.

In accordance with the act incorporating Richmond, qualified voters gathered at the Henrico County Courthouse on Main Street on Tuesday, July 2, 1782, to elect the twelve city officials who would compose the "Body Corporate" for the city. Turner Southall, a justice of the peace in Henrico County, and Gabriel Galt, an ordinary-keeper in Richmond, were responsible for holding the election and counting the ballots. Each voter was to place on the ballot the names of twelve freeholders who resided in the city. The following men were winners: Isaac Younghusband received sixty votes; William Hay, fifty-eight; James Hunter, fifty-six; Robert Mitchell, fifty-six; William Foushee, fifty-five; Richard Adams, fifty; James Buchanan, forty-nine; Samuel Sherer, forty-six; Robert Boyd, forty-three; Jacquelin Ambler, forty-one; John Beckley, thirty-nine; and John McKeand, thirty-five.

The list of inhabitants and property gathered by the city for tax purposes in 1782 indicates that the city boundaries at that time were as follows: The western boundary extended from the James River north, including both sides of First Street, to Clay Street; then east, including both sides of Clay Street, to Eighth Street; south down Eighth Street to Broad, then east on Broad to Tenth Street; south on Tenth to Grace Street; both sides of Grace, east to Twelfth Street; then continuing south to Franklin, including a small area east of Twelfth and north of Franklin; east on Franklin to Seventeenth Street; north to Broad; east on Broad to Twenty-fifth Street; and south on Twenty-fifth to the river.

On Wednesday morning, July 3, the twelve who had been elected met at the courthouse and elected William Foushee as mayor; William Hay as recorder; and Jacquelin Ambler, John Beckley, Robert Mitchell, and James Hunter, Jr., as aldermen. This left Isaac Younghusband, Richard Adams, James Buchanan, Samuel Sherer, Robert Boyd, and John McKeand as common councilmen. Turner Southall administered the oaths of office.

Fig. 20. Adam Craig House. Adam Craig was clerk of Richmond during the Revolution. His home, still standing at the corner of 19th and Grace streets, is believed to have been built in 1784. (Courtesy of the Virginia State Library.)

The Common Hall then held its first meeting, appointing Adam Craig (see fig. 20) to serve as city clerk. At its second meeting, the Common Hall unanimously elected Turner Southall as chamberlain (treasurer), divided the city into wards, and named one man in each ward to ascertain the number of inhabitants and the amount of taxable property.

The wards were as follows: Ward One, from the western extremity of the city to Eleventh Street; Ward Four, from Eleventh Street to Shockoe Creek (approximately Seventeenth Street); Ward Three, Shockoe Creek to Twenty-second Street; Ward Two, Twenty-second Street to the eastern extremity of the city.

The census takers were Jacquelin Ambler, Ward One; John Beckley, Ward Two; Robert Mitchell, Ward Three; and James Hunter, Jr., Ward Four. They were to list inhabitants by names, ages, occupations, and length of residence if less than one year preceding incorporation. Lots, improved and unimproved, were to be listed with the proprietors' names. All free mulattoes and blacks were to be listed, with their places of residence. Note was also to be made of slaves living in the city who were permitted to hire themselves out.

Shortly after the Common Hall began meeting, the Richmond hustings court organized itself and appointed additional city officials. As the third Monday had been set by law as court day, the hustings court met on Monday, July 15. Hay, recorder of the Common Hall, administered the oath of loyalty to the commonwealth to Mayor Foushee. The mayor in turn administered it to Hay and the aldermen.

Thus begun, the court of hustings then appointed Adam Craig to serve as its clerk and named the following city officials: George Richards as sergeant; Frederick Thomas, William Cooke, and Richard Bowler as constables; Stephan Tankard as public auctioneer; Robert Rawlings as clerk of the market; and Joseph Watkins as surveyor of the city. Watkins immediately got the job of ascertaining the "Limits of Jurisdiction" of the city. The court also appointed four surveyors of the streets, one for each of the four wards. Dabney Miller was to serve for Ward One, Stephen Tankard for Ward Two, Gabriel Galt for Ward Three, and Samuel Jones for Ward Four.

The new government had no place to meet regularly and no place to house people arrested in the city. But the problem was readily solved by a request to the Henrico County Court for common use of Henrico's courthouse and jail, the city to pay its due proportion of the expense of keeping these buildings in repair.

The Henrico County Court agreed, as it did to another request for the common use of the county's weights and measures, used to check the scales of merchants and warehouses. Of the five justices of peace voting on the Henrico Court when these requests were approved, one was mayor of Richmond, Foushee; one was a common councilman of the city, Younghusband; and one was its chamberlain, Turner Southall. Close ties continued between the county and the city throughout the revolutionary period.

From the first meeting in 1782 of the Common Hall through 1783, attendance and personnel turnover were problems. After missing the first two meetings of the Common Hall, Richard Adams sent his letter of resignation as common councilman. In his place the Common Hall elected Robert Brown. Isaac Younghusband resigned from the Common Hall in September 1782, and John Harvie replaced him.

After many discussions and postponements, the Common Hall adopted rules and orders governing the meetings and attendance of its members. Shortly thereafter it began fining members five shillings each time they missed a meeting without a reasonable excuse.

The May 1 meeting took action regarding Alderman James Hunter. As he had not attended for a considerable time and thus had failed to carry out the duties of his office, a summons was issued requiring him to show cause at the next meeting why he should not be suspended. The sergeant reported at the June 9 meeting that Alderman Hunter no longer resided in the city, having moved his family to another part of the state. It seems amazing that one of the four alderman in a town of less than 1,500 persons could move away without it being general knowledge!

While the Common Hall experienced chronic nonattendance during its first year, several men served with unusual faithfulness. Mitchell missed only two of the thirty-seven meetings; McKeand, four; and Buchanan, Foushee, and Hay missed only five each. Of the original twelve elected to the Common Hall, eight continued to serve at the end of the year—Foushee, Hay, Mitchell, Buchanan, Scherer, Boyd, Beckley, and McKeand.

After an abortive effort in 1782, the General Assembly at its fall session in 1783 amended the city's original charter. It enlarged the Common Hall to consist of mayor, recorder, six aldermen, and eight common councilmen.

An interesting election occurred on July 1, 1783, when the mayor's one-year term expired. On its first ballot the Common Hall elected James Buchanan to succeed Mayor Foushee. However, Buchanan turned down the job. Another ballot chose Robert Brown, but he likewise declined the position. The third choice was Alderman John Beckley, who accepted the position and immediately took the oath of office. Beckley had purchased a lot (no. 730) in Richmond just four days before the original election for the Common Hall, thus qualifying himself as a freeholder and as one who could be elected to office.

After the election of the new mayor, Common Councilman John McKeand gave a letter of resignation. Foushee was then elected to the common council in McKeand's place. At this point an election was held to replace Beckley as alderman, and Foushee was elected. Then, to replace Foushee as common councilman, the Common Hall elected John McKeand.

Thus Foushee held all three positions in the Common Hall in the same day and retained an important position in the city government and membership on the hustings court. All of this time he was also a justice on the Henrico County Court. One wonders how he had time to pursue his profession as a doctor.

The Common Hall, like the earlier town trustees, had the responsibility of regulating the construction of buildings in the city. In an apparent attempt to enhance the city's appearance, the Common Hall, in July 1782, ordered that all houses built on Main Street "shall be of the pitch of ten feet in the lower story at least exclusive of the cellar and be placed at the distance of eight feet from the Street." No new houses were to be "placed with a shed to the said Main Street, or at right angles therewith."

Three months later Common Hall passed an ordinance requiring that all "Booths or Arbours joining to any House within the City" be removed within twenty days and that no new ones be built. In the future, it decided, no "Portico, Piazza, Stairs or Steps" were to be constructed upon any part of the streets, and any in existence were to be removed within a month.

Most of the complaints to the Common Hall about buildings dealt with chimneys and the fear of fires. Earlier regulations outlawing wooden chimneys had not been enforced. The Common Hall passed an ordinance in October 1782 that stated, among other things: "Whoever shall suffer any Chimney belonging to him or her, to take fire, or shall burn straw or stubble in the Street shall forfeit and pay ten shillings for every offence. . . . " Every owner of a house with a chimney was to place a ladder on the roof near the chimney and another ladder from the ground to the roof.

This ordinance failed to settle the problem. In January 1783 Andrew Ronald, commonwealth attorney for Henrico County, issued a complaint describing as a nuisance a small house built in Serafino Formicola's garden. Buchanan and McKeand, dispatched by the Common Hall to investigate the situation, reported that the problem could be solved if Formicola repaired the roof and raised the chimney, which he agreed to do.

Another approach to controlling the problem of fires involved acquiring a fire engine. Alderman Buchanan reported to the August 20, 1782, meeting of the Common Hall that Mrs.

William Byrd had authorized him to offer a water engine belonging to her. Buchanan was designated to write Mrs. Byrd and offer her £60 for the engine if she would allow twelve months' credit.

By October 1782 the city had more than one water engine, for in an ordinance passed at that time the keeper of the water "engines" was also put in charge of having buckets made and distributed among the inhabitants. The surveyors of the streets were to dig wells and have them fitted with pumps, to be operated under their care and to be paid for out of the annual revenues of the city. At least one well was to be dug in each ward.

A company of firemen became the final step in Richmond's system of fighting fires. An ordinance of the Common Hall provided for the appointment of a captain who would recruit subordinate officers. They in turn would recruit men, up to a total of twenty. In case of fire the company would be in charge of the water engines and buckets. The officers were to set up times of practice, and the members were to be paid for their time out of the annual revenue of the city.

Putting the ordinance into effect took time, and fires continued to be a major problem. In January 1783 the Common Hall barred the use of chimneys except when it was raining. Because January and February were the coldest months in Richmond, that prohibition would surely have caused great suffering. The fire hazard in the still primarily wooden city must have been enormous for the governing body to take such drastic action.

Sanitation, a universal problem of city governments, plagued Richmond's Common Hall, too. It enacted various regulations to deal with litterers. Any person who placed "dirt or filth" from his lot into the street or onto the lot of another person was subject to a fine of one dollar. He was also to remove the offending material under penalty of paying twenty shillings for every twenty-four hours it remained.

A person was also responsible for any "dirt or filth" that collected in the street in front of his door or lot, and after the first day that person would have to pay three shillings for every day the refuse remained. A person who threw stones or rubbish into the street was subject to a five-shillings fine in the daytime, and twice that if the refuse was thrown out at night.

Outdoor toilets, referred to as "necessary houses," were to be erected at least twenty feet from the street. The owner of one already built within twenty feet of the street had a month to remove it before it was destroyed by the surveyor of streets. All necessary houses were to be cleaned every ten days during the hotter months and once every two months during the remainder of the year—but only between ten o'clock at night and sunrise the next morning. The penalty for not obeying this ordinance was a six-shillings fine for the first offense and the destruction of the house for a second offense.

The Common Hall also had to maintain streets, roads, and bridges. At an October 1782 meeting, it passed an ordinance specifying changes to be made in Main Street, from Twenty-Fifth Street to approximately Twelfth Street at Shockoe Hill. Beginning eight feet from each edge, the street was to be gradually built up to a height of two feet in the middle. A footway with a six-inch slope was to be provided on the eight-foot strip on each side of the road, so that the sloping of the entire street would provide a gentle drain for water. Holes in the streets and footways were to be filled and high places smoothed.

From the intersection of Main Street and Shockoe Hill at about Twelfth Street, a street was to be built to the top of the hill, where the capitol is today. Forty-five feet wide at its narrowest, the street would be graded like Main Street, but would have a footway on only one side. These two streets were probably the main travelways within the city.

Each landowner along the part of Main Street to be repaired was ordered to erect locust, cedar, or white-oak posts ten feet apart and nine feet from the side of the street. They were to be six inches in diameter, extending three feet into the ground and four feet above the ground, and rounded on the sides and top. If the proprietor of the land chose to paint the posts, he could do so—using white paint only.

A ford of gravel as wide as the street and firm enough for horses and carriages was to be made across Shockoe Creek. A stone bridge across the creek, and repairs to all other streets in the manner described for Main Street, had to await the availability of funds.

Further repairs were needed in March 1783. The Common Hall appointed Mayor Foushee and members Mitchell, Sherer, Boyd, and Brown to arrange with a Mr. Tait or someone else to do temporary repairs. Mayor Foushee and Alderman Beckley also met with commissioners appointed by the Henrico County Court to work out an agreement for repairing part of Main Street and the gully near John Clark's, a problem area. In August the Common Hall appointed still another committee to have the streets repaired. This time Buchanan, Brown, and Foushee were to hire laborers, and the keeper of the public jail was to employ "any hands or prisoners in his custody" for the work.

Lacking the funds to build the stone bridge needed across Shockoe Creek, the Common Hall in November 1782 petitioned the House of Delegates for state financial assistance. Alternatively, it asked for and received authorization to hold a lottery to raise money. James Tutt in Fredericksburg estimated the cost of building a stone bridge at £1,500, and a committee drew up plans for a lottery to raise that amount. But for some reason the lottery did not take place—or at any rate a permanent stone bridge was not built. The following January two Common Hall members were designated to have a temporary bridge built across Shockoe Creek.

Richmond's governing body concerned itself not only with street repair but also with traffic control and the safety of the city's pedestrians. It prohibited galloping through the streets or driving a cart or wagon at a trot or a gallop. It ruled that footways were off limits for wagons, carts, chairs, chariots, or other carriages, or for riding or tying horses. No posts were to be pulled up along the footways. Violators risked a fine of ten shillings for each offense. If the guilty person happened to be a slave or was too poor to pay the fine or to raise security within twenty-four hours, he was to receive ten lashes on the bare back.

The city faced the constant nuisance of animals running loose in its streets. An ordinance in October 1782 prohibited anyone from allowing a stallion or ridgeling to run free in the limits of the city and established a fine of forty shillings for each violation. For each hog or goat running free a fine of five shillings was to be imposed.

Hogs running free were the biggest problem, and as fines did not solve it, the Common Hall took more drastic action. The constables, after giving public notice, were instructed to seize and kill any hogs found running at large in the city and to distribute the meat among the poor.

Dead animals belonging to residents of the city posed a re-

lated problem for the government. The Common Hall passed
an ordinance in May 1783 requiring owners of horses, cattle,
and other animals that died to bury them within twelve hours in
a remote part of the city and at least three feet deep. Violators
of this ordinance were subject to a fine of twenty-four shillings.

In July 1782 the Common Hall had to resist encroachments
by persons claiming rocks, fisheries, and land that had been
considered a part of the common land belonging to the city.
The Common Hall also assumed a protective role over the
James River. In response to Philip Turpin's request, he or any
other person was given permission to blow up or remove stones
from the river opposite the commons of the city. However,
such work was to be done under the direction of Hay and
Buchanan of the Common Hall.

The Assembly granted the Common Hall powers "for im-
proving the navigation of James river, and turning Shockoe
creek into its old channel." Reported public nuisances, such as
the stone dam across the north channel of the river below
Overton's mill built by Joseph Dailey, and the fishery at Stegar's
Island, were subjects of investigation by the Common Hall.

Surprisingly, the war affected the Richmond Common Hall
only remotely from a political standpoint. Two entries in the
Common Hall records refer to hostilities directly. In the fall of
1782 the city received arms and ammunition from the state,
which the Common Hall assigned to be distributed by Capts.
Robert Mitchell and John Brooke. At news of the ending of
the war, the Common Hall passed the following resolution:

Whereupon it is ordered that the Serjeant at the Hour of 10 o'clock
tomorrow morning do give public notice by a beat of the Drum
through the City that Proclamation for a Cessation of Hostilities will
be proclaimed at the hour of 12 in the most public places of the City,
to wit, at the Courthouse, market square & at the foot of Shockoe Hill.
That the Serjeant in proclaiming the same, be mounted on Horseback
& that the Constables of the City with staves do attend him on foot to
preserve Order and Decorum.

CHAPTER FIVE

The British Are Coming!

ALTHOUGH the Matthews-Collier expedition of May 1779 into Hampton Roads had helped push the capital from Williamsburg to Richmond, it did nothing for Virginia's defense posture. As soon as the British raiding force withdrew, Governor Henry ordered the militia disbanded: "The enemy are gone to sea," he told Col. Theodorick Bland. "You will discharge the militia as soon as you judge it proper. Their affairs, I guess, press hard for their return home."

For the next year and a half Virginia seemed immune to the fighting taking place elsewhere in the colonies, but the defeat of General Gates at Camden, South Carolina, brought a sense of insecurity to Richmonders.

After the battle, the victorious Cornwallis (see fig. 21) dispatched Maj. Patrick Ferguson and a British force toward Virginia. Even though Ferguson's force was crushed at King's Mountain, South Carolina, the British evidently intended to make Virginia their key to subduing the southern states.

While Cornwallis was invading the western Carolinas, General Clinton dispatched a large naval expedition under Gen. Alexander Leslie from New York to the Chesapeake. It was to be a diversionary effort. Clinton instructed Leslie "to proceed up James River as high as possible, in order to seize or destroy any magazines the enemy may have at Petersburgh, Richmond, or any of the places adjacent." Then he was to establish a post on the Elizabeth River, there to await orders from Cornwallis.

With more than 2,500 men, Leslie arrived at the mouth of the James on October 15, 1780, and debarked at Portsmouth. This time Virginia had some militia in readiness. Governor Jefferson, receiving word of the debarkation in the morning of October 22, directed all forces in the Portsmouth area to serve under the command of Gen. George Weedon until the fighting parson, Gen. Peter Muhlenberg, should arrive. Muhlenberg soon appeared. With several thousand troops he took a defense

GENERAL BENEDICT ARNOLD IN 1778.

Fig. 21. Lord Cornwallis. Tactical errors in Virginia caused him to be trapped at Yorktown, which cost the British the war. (Courtesy of the National Archives.)

Fig. 22. General Benedict Arnold (drawn by DuSimetiere, originally published May 1783). Arnold raided and burned Richmond in early January 1781. (Courtesy of the Virginia State Library.)

Fig. 23. Major General William Phillips. Phillips was an artillery-trained officer who took command in Virginia in April 1781. He died in Petersburg in May 1781, where he is buried. (Courtesy of the National Archives.)

Fig. 24. Banastre Tarleton. Tarleton came to Virginia with Cornwallis in 1781, and made two long, but relatively useless, raids into western Virginia. He surrendered at Yorktown. (Courtesy of the National Archives.)

line around Portsmouth and gradually drove in the enemy's picket lines.

Leslie, who had initially advanced as far as Smithfield, did not want to risk a battle. He was determined, however, to make a stand in Portsmouth, and there the British "covered themselves with the most intricate defiles."

The possibility remained that the enemy might break out and march on the capital. Few legislators stayed in Richmond during the crisis—not enough to make a quorum, "altho the invasion of our country calls loudly for legislative aid." Yet, wrote Richard Henry Lee from Richmond, "Great spirit appears among the people of all ranks and much zeal to engage the enemy, but the extensiveness of the country and dispersion of the people occasion delay." Another difficulty arose from the artillery and small arms not being "in proper order."

Suddenly, on November 15, the enemy embarked. It was supposed they would proceed up the James River. Muhlenberg, accordingly, took his army higher up the river in order to observe their movement. After hovering offshore a few days, Leslie set out for Charleston, from where he would march overland to join Cornwallis. In Virginia, most of the militia again packed up and went home; those having enlisted for service in the field from six to eighteen months made ready to join the Southern Army.

While the enemy was taking leave of Virginia, two generals— Greene and Steuben—"with their suite" arrived in Richmond on November 16. Greene, newly appointed commander of the Southern Army, stayed in Richmond five days, where he enjoyed the cordiality of Jefferson, and then journeyed southward to assume command of his army.

Before leaving Richmond, Greene designated General Steuben as commander in chief of the armed forces in Virginia (see fig. 31).

Steuben formally took command on December 3, with Muhlenberg now second in command. Hardly had Steuben begun to take stock of the military situation and to follow through on his major responsibility of arranging troops and supplies for the Southern Army, when another British invasion struck in Virginia at the end of the month.

Unknown to Virginians, twenty-seven British ships had set out from New York on December 20. They carried an expeditionary force, consisting mainly of the loyalist Queen's Rangers and New York volunteers, commanded by Benedict Arnold (see fig. 22). Arnold had the same instructions as Leslie, except that Arnold's specified the establishment of a strong post at Portsmouth. He was to concentrate on the destruction of munitions and materiel that could be used by the Southern Army.

Arnold eagerly anticipated the opportunity to employ his military skills for the first time in three years and to share in the spoils of war, which British practice allowed. Clinton, who did not fully trust the traitorous hero, ordered him to consult on all decisions with two subordinates, Lt. Col. John Graves Simcoe and Lt. Col. Thomas Dundas.

Arnold's flotilla reached Hampton Roads on December 30. With his usual penchant for swift action, Arnold gave orders to sail immediately up the James. Forcing the poorly defended narrows at Hood's Point, Arnold disembarked at Westover, about twenty-five miles from Richmond, on January 4, 1781. He spared only a few moments to exchange amenities with the proprietress of the plantation, his widowed cousin-in-law Mrs. Byrd. Word came that a force was gathering at Richmond.

Arnold hesitated to pursue his objective of a raid on Richmond, since he had been ordered not to take any great risk. He was well aware that his small striking force, however seasoned, would be no match for an aroused countryside, where thousands could turn out to oppose him. As the most wanted criminal in America, he knew that, if captured, the highest gibbet in the land awaited him. But his seconds-in-command, Lieutenant Colonels Dundas and Simcoe, advised that a one-day march to Richmond could be made "with perfect security," and Arnold was always a man of daring.

The invasion caught the Virginia government entirely unprepared. Jefferson first learned of the British arrival in the Chesapeake on Sunday, New Year's Eve, but deferred any action until he could learn whether the fleet was British or French and where it was headed. Word reached Jefferson on Tuesday morning that British transports had entered the James River. Immediately he called a meeting of the Council of State, with General Steuben attending. The legislators in town acted as couriers, carrying circular letters to the county lieutenants in their respective counties. All ablebodied men were called up in

Henrico, Chesterfield, Hanover, Goochland, and Powhatan counties, and from one-fourth to one-half of the militia from sixteen other counties. All of the 4,600 militiamen summoned were to be placed under General Steuben.

Jefferson thought that Arnold's first objective would be Williamsburg. But late on January 4 the startling news came that the enemy had landed at Westover and was on the way to Richmond. For two days, January 2–4, Jefferson had worked feverishly to get public stores and documents out of Richmond and Westham. George Muter, in charge of the War Office in Richmond, rounded up all the supplies he could find and sent them across the river to Manchester.

After dark on the fourth Jefferson rode up to the Westham foundry. On his way he met Daniel Hylton of Henrico, who was on his way to join the militia. Jefferson asked Hylton to supervise the removal of powder, arms, and munitions across the river. Jefferson himself stayed at Hylton's house near Westham until midnight, sending his family eight miles up the river to Tuckahoe, where he joined them early Friday morning.

Sending his family another eight miles up to Fine Creek the next morning, Jefferson crossed the river from Westham, hoping to confer with Steuben. He finally caught up with the general at Col. William Fleming's in Powhatan County (near Midlothian). There the governor received a proposal from Arnold for ransoming the safety of Richmond—at least that was implicit in Arnold's letter. (See fig. 25.) If Richmonders would surrender the town without resistance, the British would only take away the tobacco stored there. Jefferson refused the offer. Arnold apparently approached General Steuben with the same proposal, but the baron would not receive the emissary.

Meanwhile, during the afternoon of the fourth, Arnold advanced toward Richmond by the Darbytown Road. Halting at Fourmile Creek, twelve miles from the town, his troops encamped for the night.

Several hundred militiamen were now pouring into Manchester from Henrico and Chesterfield counties. In Richmond only about a hundred had appeared, with a few more still coming in. Many had no arms, because weapons in Richmond had been taken across the river to Manchester. General Steuben ordered the militia in Richmond to march toward Ar-

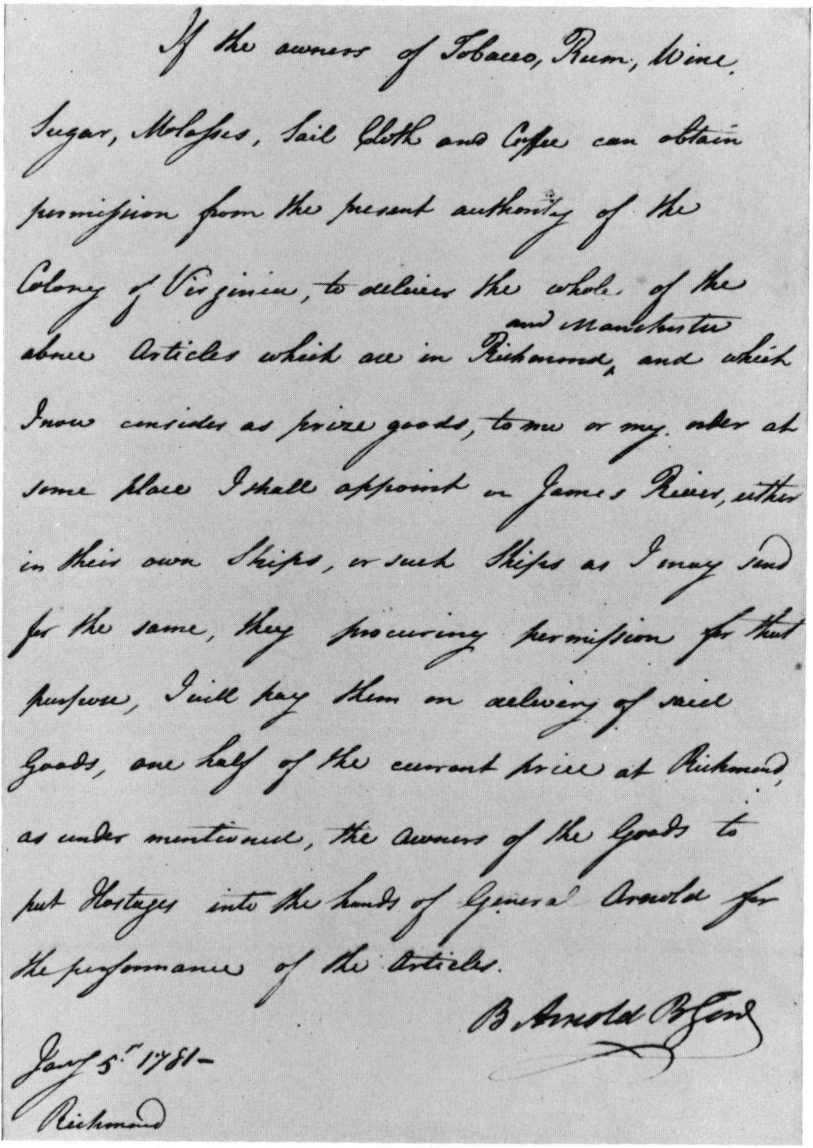

If the owners of Tobacco, Rum, Wine, Sugar, Molasses, Sail Cloth and Coffee can obtain permission from the present authority of the Colony of Virginia, to deliver the whole of the above Articles which are in Richmond and Manchester, and which I now consider as prize goods, to me or my order at some place I shall appoint on James River, either in their own Ships, or such Ships as I may send for the same, they procuring permission for that purpose, I will pay them on delivery of said Goods, one half of the current price at Richmond, as under mentioned, the Owners of the Goods to put Hostages into the hands of General Arnold for the performance of the Articles.

B Arnold B Genl

Jany 5th 1781–
Richmond

Fig. 25. Benedict Arnold's proposal to the inhabitants of Richmond and Manchester, January 7, 1781. (Courtesy of the Virginia Historical Society.)

nold's force. On making contact, they were to fire one volley, then retreat directly back to Richmond. Maj. Alexander Dick, a capable and ambitious officer from Fredericksburg, commanded this little force.

Dick and the militia left Richmond late in the evening of the fourth. The major did not know the terrain and had received poor intelligence. For twenty-four hours the militia stumbled through woods and swamps, always in retreat, never firing a shot at the enemy. Conflicting and inaccurate reports made matters worse.

Finally, Major Dick and his men retreated all the way to Richmond Hill (now Church Hill), which they thought would be too steep for Colonel Simcoe's cavalry.

Shortly after noon on January 5, the two to three hundred Americans on the hill spotted the first file of British soldiers on the road below. Arnold has his troops strung out, in order to give the impression of great numbers. Colonel Simcoe (see fig. 26) received permission from Arnold to attack the hill, although Arnold said it would not be worth the effort, because the militia would not fight.

Fig. 26. John Graves Simcoe. He commanded the Queen's Rangers, who raided through Richmond in 1781. (Courtesy of the Virginia State Library.)

In ascending the hill, Simcoe and his cavalry dismounted and led their horses. The Americans did not even fire, according to the British version of the attack. The recently discovered diary of a Hessian officer, however, credits the defenders with a single volley. At any rate, the militia fled several miles into the woods.

While Simcoe was putting the Americans on Richmond Hill to the test, Colonel Dundas led the main British force into the lower town. A small party of Americans on horseback pulled back across Shockoe Creek and up Shockoe Hill to join others on the hill. Simcoe's cavalry, crossing Richmond Hill almost unnoticed, planned to descend to the rear of the American horsemen. Hardly any signs of life remained in the lower town, however. But on top of Shockoe Hill waited a great number of Americans on horseback, "made up of militia, [and] spectators, some with and some without arms."

Simcoe's rangers galloped up the hill, and the group of mounted militia and spectators fled in every direction through the woods. Colonel Simcoe and Captain Shank pursued them four or five miles but only managed to take a half-dozen captives. Again, the sight of precision-trained combat troops had terrified the would-be defenders, most of whom had guns unfit for use.

It was to be a long day for Lt. Col. John Graves Simcoe (see fig. 27). Already, after a half-day's march, he had assaulted the enemy on two steep hills and had dispersed them. Now Arnold had another assignment for him. He dispatched Simcoe and four hundred men—his rangers and the "flank companies of the 80th" under Major Gordon—to destroy the munitions and foundry at Westham, seven miles up the river. Setting out in midafternoon, Simcoe and his men reached the foundry just before dusk. About three hundred militia "had arrived at Westham on their way down, and arms were actually recrossing for them, but hearing of the Enemy's approach and being without Arms, they dispersed."

In a crippling stroke, Simcoe destroyed a large quantity of small arms and military stores and broke off the trunnions of the cannon. He had originally intended to blow up the magazine, but that being too dangerous, he had the powder carried down the cliffs and poured into the river. He set afire

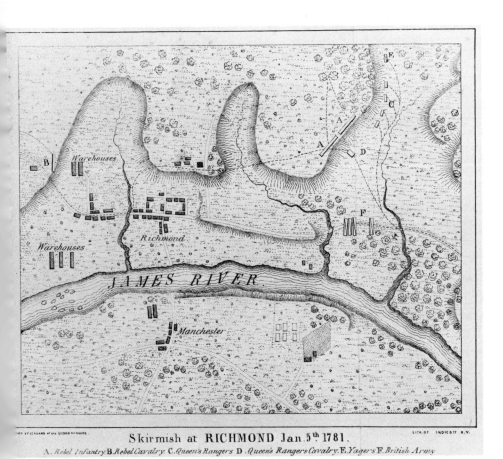

Skirmish at **RICHMOND** Jan.5th 1781.

A. *Rebel Infantry* B.*Rebel Cavalry.* C.*Queen's Rangers* D .*Queen's Rangers Cavalry.* E.*Yagers* F.*British Army*

Fig. 27. Skirmish at Richmond. This map was drawn by one of Simcoe's officers. Reproduced from Simcoe's *Journal*. (Courtesy of the Virginia State Library.)

the boring mill, the magazine, the ordnance repair shop, John Ballendine's house, and one or two warehouses. Some of the state documents that had been brought to Westham also went up in flames. Fortunately, only the roof of the foundry burned, and its chimneys remained intact.

Simcoe's excursionary force returned to Richmond the same evening. Some of the troops were already bedded down. Arnold and Simcoe spent the evening in Galt's Tavern. Many British soldiers, too exhausted to sleep, went out on liberty of the town. Largely "special forces"—rangers and Germans— they were not subject to the usual martinet discipline in the British army. And since Arnold and Simcoe depended for the success of the mission on the high spirits of their troops, neither officer wished to dampen morale.

During the night soldiers combed the town looking for liquor. Even British pickets posted beyond the town found time to indulge in drink. William Tatham, sent by General Nelson during the invasion to find Governor Jefferson, stopped just outside of town at Samuel DuVal's house at Mount Comfort. The enemy's pickets had been there, and Tatham found "the floor was flowing with the Liquors spilt by the British soldiers."

Writing from Farmingdale two weeks after Arnold's occupation, St. George Tucker lamented, as one of "the calamities of war," his loss of rum in Richmond, though "it was too trifling a quantity for a man to break his heart about, being only two hogsheads."

Even though the British soldiers rummaged through the empty dwellings of the majority of the white citizenry who had fled the town, they engaged in no large-scale pilferage of personal property. Plundering was strictly forbidden by both the British and American armies. Yet "straggling parties" of the British soldiery seem to have done some looting as they marched from Richmond to Westover the following day.

Arnold himself left the tobacco in the town untouched. He may have calculated that he would be commanding a British army in Virginia for some time to come, and that he might have a chance to intercept tobacco sent down the river from Richmond later and could then share in the spoils. Whatever the reason, leaving the tobacco untouched could not have been an oversight.

Yet British depredations in Richmond proved extensive. Less than two hours before the British were to leave Richmond, they set fire to several public buildings, the ropewalk, warehouses, and workshops. Windswept fires destroyed several houses and one of the town's two printing presses. Arnold spared the capitol, probably because he did not recognize the old warehouse as the seat of government, but possibly because he knew it was property of the British-owned William Cuninghame and Company.

Just after noon of the sixth, exactly twenty-four hours after he had entered Richmond, Arnold led his troops out of town, back toward Westover. Behind them a great cloud of smoke rose from the town; provisions and liquors were strewn all about the streets. Without any doubt, the enemy had made his presence felt.

The day after Arnold left Richmond, citizens began to return. But several days passed before law and order could be restored. Negroes of the town allegedly "committed great Ravages," burning one house at night and plundering and hiding public stores. Maj. Richard Claiborne, the deputy quartermaster general of the state, secured a party of militia from Colonel Haskins, which he used to patrol the streets at night.

Claiborne found reason to complain of these militia as a police force: "I am sorry that the Militia differ so much from the Contl. Soldiers, but by constant watch I kept them alert, and constantly at their duty." The return of Jefferson to Richmond on January 8, and thereafter of other state officials, helped to restore the visible presence of authority.

Americans themselves, both white and black, probably did most of the looting of the town in the period just after the British withdrew. In any case, losses were great. The auditor's books, treasurer's records, county records, and money were missing, even though allegedly Arnold had not destroyed them. James Madison's father, in Richmond a week or so after the invasion, reported, however, that the British had ruined "every Thing they could lay their Hands upon."

One depredation was painfully evident: many slaves had left with Arnold. There was also injured pride. Jefferson, infuriated when he learned that Arnold had donated twenty guineas for aid to the poor to James Buchanan, a Richmond merchant, peremptorily ordered Buchanan to return the money to Arnold.

As Richmond healed its wounds, the people awoke to the shocking reality that the war indeed had come to Virginia. The enemy had raided at will, without, as General Steuben himself said, a single shot being fired, not even in defense of the capital.

The disbelief was none the less in the North. Wrote Ralph Izard from Philadelphia: "Arnold's success against Richmond appears very extraordinary." Leslie's invasion should "have put Virginia more on her guard, than to suffer such an insult, as she has lately received, with impunity."

Jefferson must come in for a large share of the blame. He did not believe the British intended, or were capable of, a sudden penetration into the state. Overconfident, he thought ample resources of manpower existed to thwart any invasion. The outcome of the British invasion might have been entirely different if Jefferson had issued a militia call a few days before he did. As his correspondence reveals, however, Jefferson, at the time of the invasion, was mainly concerned with the war in the west.

Others share the blame. But chiefly the fault lay in an inadequate command system, overlapping authority, poor communication, and ignorance of the terrain east of Richmond by officers in the field.

Why did the Americans not at least fire on the British? Again, the inadequate arms. But more importantly, if the militia had stood to fire, by the time they could have reloaded the enemy would have been upon them. Such a pause might even have meant capture. The defenders of Richmond acted as if not annoying the enemy would encourage him to go away.

Psychologically the Virginians, long apathetic toward a distant war, lacked instant motivation. But whatever the reasons for Arnold's brilliant success against Richmond, this was not Virginia's finest hour. Not until the British were ready to return down the James did resistance show up.

This time the enemy had come to stay in Virginia. Arnold's troops were entrenched in Portsmouth and clearly intended to make that town a permanent base of operations.

In view of the expansion of the war in the South and the

disastrous performance of the Virginia militia during Arnold's raid, Washington decided to send a Continental force to Virginia, at least temporarily. He hoped to discourage further forays by Arnold's force and also any idea Cornwallis might have of striking out for Virginia. The presence of a sizable Continental detachment, he expected, would hearten the war effort within the state.

Washington's young protégé, the marquis de Lafayette (see fig. 28), solicited Washington for the command of an army in Virginia. Now twenty-three years old and entering his fourth year as a major general, the marquis chafed at the long inaction of the northern army and the cancellation of an invasion of Canada that he was to have led. He welcomed an opportunity to win the laurels of victory in the field.

The chance to become the "Commander General in Virginia of the American troops" was not long in coming. On February 20, 1781, Washington ordered Lafayette into action at once. He was to lead an "expedition to Virginia against Arnold," consisting of three battalions of light infantry from the New England and the New Jersey troops.

Lafayette left immediately from Washington's encampment at New Windsor, Connecticut, assembled his troops at Peekskill, New York, and marched to Philadelphia. There he spent a week in arranging for supplies. Lafayette's detachment of 1,200 men finally arrived at Yorktown on March 14. After visiting with Steuben at Williamsburg and being pleased with the preparations that Steuben was making, Lafayette marched his men to Suffolk to join General Muhlenberg, whose militia faced the British at Portsmouth.

Lafayette convinced himself that Muhlenberg's one thousand-man force, though chiefly made up of three-months militia, could keep the enemy contained. So he returned overland to Maryland to await further instructions from Washington. Leaving Williamsburg on March 28, Lafayette's little army may have passed through Richmond as it headed northward through Fredericksburg and Mount Vernon.

While Lafayette had taken leave of Virginia, General William Phillips (see fig. 23), familiar with Virginia from his detention as a prisoner of war but recently exchanged, arrived at Portsmouth. He commanded twenty-three transports, capable of

Fig. 28.   Marquis de Lafayette after the American Revolution. This painting
is presently in the Valentine Museum, Richmond, Virginia. (Courtesy of the
Valentine Museum, Richmond, Va.)

carrying 150–200 men each. Phillips's reinforcement brought the British army at Portsmouth to about 4,500, the highest estimate. Opposing this army at Suffolk, twenty-six miles away, Muhlenberg had about one thousand militia.

When Washington learned of Phillips's landing, he instructed Lafayette to return to Virginia as a commander, under General Greene and at Greene's further discretion, of all troops in Virginia. Steuben accepted Washington's orders without protest.

Lafayette stayed nearly a month in Maryland, collecting supplies, securing a loan of £2,000 sterling from Baltimore merchants, and prevailing on the ladies of Baltimore to make summer clothes for the army. On April 14 he wrote the French minister to the United States: "I am on my way and the Susquehana has been my Rubicon; I am going to run after General Phillips but I do not hope to catch him." Actually he did not leave Annapolis until April 20, two days after Phillips led an expedition out of Portsmouth.

Lafayette's forced march to Virginia took him through Bladensburg, Georgetown, Alexandria, Colchester, Dumfries, Fredericksburg, Bowling Green, and Hanover Court House. Lafayette's army arrived at Richmond about five o'clock on Sunday evening, April 29. The troops were immediately quartered in the ropewalk at the east end of town. The next day the American force moved to the heights of Richmond to await Phillips's army. (See figs. 29 and 30.)

General Phillips had several options once he left Portsmouth: to raid quickly towards Richmond and return to Portsmouth; to march to North Carolina and join Cornwallis; or, should Cornwallis decide to join him, to remain in the field in Virginia to effect a junction.

From April 18 to 24 Phillips's invasion force, using only the smallest vessels of the fleet, moved up the James River. His immediate objectives were to disperse militia assembled at Williamsburg and to destroy American stores on the south side of the James that had been untouched by Arnold's invasion. When the invasion force landed at City Point late on the twenty-fourth, it became obvious that the British intended to advance along the south side of the river to Petersburg and Richmond.

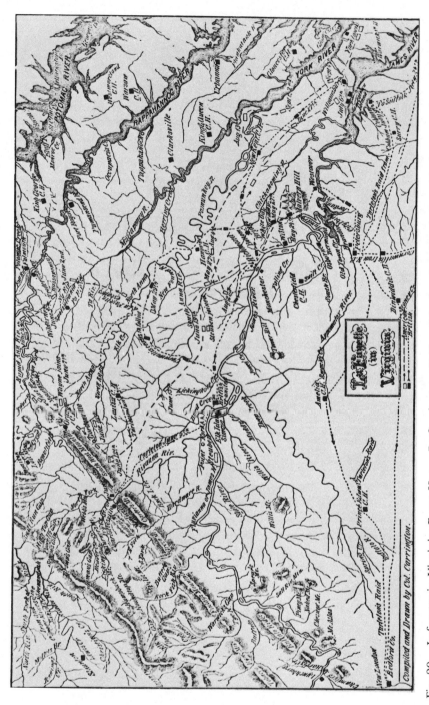

Fig. 29. Lafayette in Virginia. From Henry B. Carrington, *Battles of the American Revolution, 1775–81*, this map shows operations in eastern Virginia, 1781. (Reproduced by the Virginia State Library.)

Fig. 30. James Armistead Lafayette. A slave from the Richmond area who served as a courier and spy for Lafayette, through Lafayette's recommendation he was freed by the Virginia Assembly after the war. (Courtesy of the Valentine Museum, Richmond, Va.)

Scarcely two months had passed since the humiliation of Arnold's depredations, and now another British army had descended on central Virginia to finish the job. Governor Jefferson had again been caught off guard. But this time Virginians were determined to vindicate their honor against the enemy.

On the nineteenth, Jefferson and the Council, "having received Intelligence that the Enemy are in Motion up James River . . . and their destination being as yet unknown," ordered all the militia of Hanover, Henrico, Goochland, Dinwiddie, and Prince George counties to come to Richmond as speedily as possible. They should "not wait to come altogether, but repair here in parties as they can be collected." All the Powhatan County militia were to muster at Manchester. One half of the Cumberland and Amelia militia were ordered to Richmond.

"Former experience," Jefferson noted, should "induce a more prompt Attendance on this Occasion." In the event of "a very rapid movement of the enemy" towards Richmond, the Goochland, Hanover, and Powhatan militia should rendezvous at the Manakin Town ferry, and the Cumberland militia at the same place or at Manchester. In such an emergency the Amelia militia were to meet at Petersburg or along the Appomattox River, the Chesterfield County militia at Petersburg and Manchester.

Jefferson himself made preparations to remove the public papers from Richmond. During the next four days only about four hundred militia cavalry and infantry had gathered at Manchester and Richmond, more than half of them unarmed. Jefferson, disappointed at the poor turnout, gave the command of these troops to Col. James Wood, pending further orders from Steuben. "This fatal Tardiness," he wrote, "will I fear be as unfortunate for Williamsburg on this Occasion as formerly it was for Richmond."

During the period from April 19 to 24, while General Phillips's intentions remained unclear, Muhlenberg and Steuben were not inactive. They attempted to prepare for the British as best they could, meanwhile gathering men and matériel in Petersburg. An all-day engagement there on the twenty-fifth failed to stem the British advance, however.

Outnumbered, outgunned, and outgeneraled, Steuben beat a zigzag retreat through Chesterfield County and eventually to Richmond. A British detachment under Arnold captured or demolished most of the ships in Virginia's navy as they lay at anchor in the James. And Phillips pressed on. Reaching Manchester, he burned 1,200 hogsheads of tobacco, some public buildings, "plundered the inhabitants of their furniture, killed a large number of cattle, hogs, &c." Next Phillips planned to take Richmond. But his luck had run out.

On the thirtieth, having secured the craft to take his troops across the river to Richmond, Phillips gave the signal for attack. But at that moment, about dusk, he scanned the steep hill overlooking the north bank. What he saw made him fly "into a violent passion." Silhouetted against the skyline on top of Richmond Hill was an American army of nearly 3,300 troops—Lafayette's Continentals, 2,000 militia, and 60 dragoons.

Some of Phillips's men were already landing across the river, but a militia charge drove them back to their boats. Because of the large American army and the advantage they held for using artillery, Phillips decided not to risk attacking Richmond. It is said that he swore an oath of vengeance against Lafayette for denying him the prize.

Lafayette afterwards commented that the American show of force "put these cowardly plunderers under way down the River." Yet, the gathering American force had watched as "quiet spectators" while the British wreaked destruction in Manchester. Phillips accomplished his mission even if he could not deliver the crowning blow of taking the capital.

To the Americans, the defense of Richmond was a victory without a battle. But they had no time for joyous celebration; the British invasion army was still operating with strength not far away. The day after Phillips withdrew from across the river "the army was paraded on a large plain," just northwest of Richmond (probably in the vicinity of what is now Belvidere Street).

The next day, which was "exceedingly warm," Lafayette planned his strategy. He would march towards the British army at a cautious distance. Should Phillips move to Williamsburg, as the marquis expected, "there to collect Contributions which he had imposed," then Lafayette planned to take a position between the Pamunkey and Chickahominy rivers. So poised, he could cover Richmond as well as "some other interesting parts of the State."

The American soldiers in Richmond were ordered to cut their coats short to give them greater mobility. Other preparations went forward to pursue the enemy. Nevertheless, the officers did find time to help Major Reed celebrate his birthday with "a cold cut and drink of grog with him at an elegant spring," a half mile north of town.

At daylight on the third, the army moved to Bottoms Bridge on the Chickahominy, fifteen miles east of Richmond, and encamped in a thick woods. Lafayette kept his troops in this area for four days. The enemy had not withdrawn farther down the river, and perhaps they would head back up the river before striking southward to join Cornwallis.

Lafayette wrote his commander in chief to justify his caution because of the lack of boats, wagons, and spies, and the undependability of the militia. Phillips had "every advantage" over him, and "a defeat would have scattered the militia, lost the few arms we have and knocked down this handfull of Continental troops."

As for the defense of Richmond, Lafayette told Washington:

I did not know but what the enemy meant to establish a post. Under the circumstances I thought it better to fight on none but my own grounds, and to defeat the main and most valuable object of the enemy. Had I gone on the other side, the ennemy would have given me the slip and taken Richmond, leaving nothing to me but the reputation of a rash unexperienced young man. Our stores could not be removed.

To General Jethro Sumner of North Carolina, Lafayette wrote, "Our Business is . . . to divide the Enemy and prevent a junction of Phillips and Cornwallis." But he was not strong enough to do so. After moving down the James River, Phillips did come back toward the west to await at Petersburg the arrival of Cornwallis. Lafayette shifted ground accordingly, encamping and watchfully waiting at Wilton.

There, on May 16, the marquis received two items of news: General Phillips had died, and General Cornwallis had crossed the Roanoke River into Virginia. After being ill for two weeks and unconscious for several days, Phillips died from what is generally thought to have been yellow fever. His grave, left unmarked in the Blandford Church yard so that Americans could not desecrate it, has not been found to this day.

Cornwallis reached Petersburg on May 20 and thereby "formed a junction with the corps under Arnold," who had succeeded Phillips. When Cornwallis arrived and assumed command, Arnold requested and received permission to return to New York. His service as a field commander in Virginia, however, would not be without its material reward. Laying claim to one-eighth of the spoils from the many British raids, Arnold would realize £2,068—the amount on record—and probably more.

Lafayette learned of the junction of the two British armies the same day that it occurred. After having his troops perform a "sham battle," he led them to Richmond, arriving there late in the evening of May 20. Again the soldiers took up quarters in the ropewalk.

Virginia was evidently becoming the major testing ground of

Fig. 31. Baron von Steuben. Steuben was inspector general of the Continental army and commander in chief of forces in Virginia. This photo was taken from the original in Independence Hall, Philadelphia, by C. W. Peale. (Courtesy of the Valentine Museum, Richmond, Va.)

Fig. 32. General Anthony Wayne. Wayne commanded the Pennsylvania troops reinforcing Lafayette in Virginia. (Courtesy of the Detroit Historical Society.)

the Revolution. A British reinforcement of 2,000 troops would soon land at Portsmouth. The British commander in Virginia would then have over 7,000 men at his disposal—the third-largest field concentration of British strength during the war.

At Richmond, Lafayette cautiously awaited the next British move. He could hardly afford to take the war to Cornwallis. He had only 900 Continentals and could only discount the militia, who "are not numerous, come without arms, and are not used to war." General Anthony Wayne's detachment of Pennsylvanians, whom Washington had ordered to Virginia—long delayed by commissary problems—still had not arrived. (See fig. 32.) Lafayette reckoned that the British outnumbered his infantry five to one and his cavalry ten to one.

Whenever the Pennsylvanians under Wayne should arrive, and when more of the militia turned out, Lafayette considered striking the British one blow. "Being Beat," he wrote, "I may at least Be Beat with some decency." But until his force could be substantially enlarged, Lafayette decided on limited skirmishing, and "particularly to take care against their immense and excellent body of horse, whom the militia fears as they would so many wild beasts."

Cornwallis, however, had the same immediate objective as had Arnold and Phillips: to destroy supplies, manufactories, and warehouses in Virginia, and thereby to cut off the sources of supplies to the armies of both Lafayette and Greene. If he succeeded in defeating Lafayette while raiding throughout Virginia, all the better. Writing to Clinton, Cornwallis outlined his plan: "I shall now proceed to dislodge La Fayette from Richmond, and with my light troops to destroy any magazines or stores in the neighbourhood. . . ." Then he would move to "the neck at Williamsburgh . . . and keep myself unengaged from operations which might interfere with your plan for the campaign until I have the satisfaction of hearing from you." Cornwallis also suggested that Yorktown would be a better base than Portsmouth.

Having gotten his army across the James at City Point and received the regiment just landed at Portsmouth, Cornwallis began his campaign. On May 27 the British army encamped near White Oak Swamp and the next day at Bottoms Bridge. Cornwallis planned to take Richmond from the rear. But learning that Lafayette had already evacuated the city, he swung his army around Richmond in order to follow closely the marquis's retreat northward. Most Richmonders fled upon news of Cornwallis's advance.

Through the next fourteen days the two forces maneuvered—never facing each other—while the cavalry of Tarleton (see fig. 24) and Simcoe ranged far and wide destroying stores and facilities. At last, on June 10, Anthony Wayne arrived at Lafayette's encampment at Raccoon Ford with nine hundred troops—three regiments of Pennsylvania Continentals and one hundred Continental artillerymen. It was now Lafayette's turn to pursue the British.

Cornwallis had left Elk Hill for Richmond on June 15 and entered the town the following day. Because he had "in vain endeavoured to bring the Marquis to action" and had "destroyed all the Stores within my reach," he decided to move on to Williamsburg and establish a post there. During the night of June 20, Cornwallis evacuated Richmond.

While in Richmond, the British set fire to "a number of houses" as well as to about two thousand hogsheads of tobacco, which they piled in the streets. They also destroyed various stores and supplies, including salt, harnesses, uniforms, five thousand muskets, and six hundred bushels of flour.

Lafayette learned the next day of Cornwallis's departure. Immediately he set out for Richmond, and about seven o'clock in the evening of June 21 the army halted on "a plain" north of the town. Whether Lafayette proceeded through the town proper the next morning is subject to some question. Captain John Davis noted that twenty-four hours after the enemy left Richmond, Lafayette's army marched through the town, and "it appears a scene of much distress." Daniel Trabue was more enthusiastic: "a little after sunrise, General Lafayette marched through the town with his army; each man's hat contained a green bush. I thought it was the prettiest sight I had ever seen."

Lieutenant Ebenezer Wild, however, said that the army took "a back road (as the enemy had left the small pox in town)" and "marched five miles, and halted in Bottoms Bridge road, two miles below Richmond, where we remained all night."

If the army appeared to be in a hurry, at least there was leisure time in the afternoon of June 22. Captain Davis and Lieutenant Feltman went to Richmond "and spent the afternoon playing billiards and drinking wine." They did not seem to mind that the village was all but a ghost town. Further troop movements leading to the surrender at Yorktown hardly affected Richmond. Nor did the passage through the town of French and Continental regiments returning northward or heading southward after Yorktown. Once again life could become normal in the state's capital.

Richmonders returned to business as usual as they sought to recuperate from the British depredations. The politicians had come back, and the legislature, reconvening in early November, could now proceed without fear of disruption. Evidences of the war remained, of course. The government struggled to finance both the declining costs of operations and growing veterans' claims. Moreover, for better or for worse, Richmond continued for some time to house a complicated and often ineffective military bureaucracy.

CHAPTER SIX

A Hub of Army Supply

VIRGINIANS had long since discovered that making war required a lot more than simply going off to battle. Then as now, men in the field depended on a supporting network of people and facilities to provide recruits, arms and equipment, food, clothing, pay, medical care, transportation, and custody of enemy prisoners of war. Having to support both the Continental army and the state militia raised further complications.

Before 1780, procurement was largely a matter of local merchants selling to the government supplies that came into their hands. District agents, subquartermasters, and commissaries supervised the process on the government side. About the only significant staff official before that time was the commissary of stores. When the capital was moved, Richmond became the staff headquarters in Virginia, which brought to town the military bureaucracy and all the confusion inherent in the overlapping of the various departments.

The move from Williamsburg brought to an end the boards of trade, war, and navy, which had existed less than a year. In their place the Assembly in May 1780 created the offices of commissioner of war and commissioner of the navy, naming to them Col. George Muter and Capt. James Maxwell, respectively. Thomas Smith continued in the office of commercial agent, which now took on a new importance.

The most important office of the revised war administration was that of commissioner of war. George Muter proved inefficient and Col. William Davies replaced him on March 22, 1781. Davies, the son of the Great Awakening divine, Samuel Davies, was a superb administrator and perhaps the ablest man in the Virginia government. As Virginia's commissioner of war, he directed all facets of the war effort.

In Richmond, Davies made his office in "the Senate House." The commissary of stores used the house of Miles Selden, Jr. The houses of Thomas Prosser, James Lyle, and Richard

Adams served as the offices of the quartermaster department (moved to Richmond in December 1780) and also for "public stores of different kinds."

Thomas Smith became security "for the rent of a house in the city of Richmond for the use of the quartermasters department" and was "threatened with a suit at law for the same." Smith asked the governor to "exonerate him therefrom," but no money was available and he then petitioned the legislature for relief. Three other houses, belonging to James Buchanan, Thompson Mason, and George Nicholas, were used as "public workshops." Arnold destroyed the houses containing the military stores.

Exact location of the clothier and naval offices is not known. Nor is it known whether any buildings were specially constructed for the military offices, although the town's leading citizens met at Hogg's Tavern as early as July 1779 to draw up plans for such a possibility. Some staff officers were not so fortunate in finding accommodations. Deputy Quartermaster General William Finnie had tried "to fix myself at Richmond," but could not find a house.

The location of the "Public Store" of the quartermaster department, after it was moved from Williamsburg to Richmond in 1781, cannot be determined. It may have been in one of the above-mentioned houses; or—because there is no evidence that it was in the city proper—it may have been as far as a few miles outside of Richmond.

The quartermaster department had overall supervision of army supply and often got involved in the particular matters of the other supply departments. Its main area of direct responsibility was transportation.

Although the Committee of Safety named William Finnie quartermaster general in 1775, most state quartermaster matters were handled by the commissary of public stores. General authority was exercised by the Council until 1779 and by the boards of trade, war, and navy in 1779–80.

Since the war, after the opening phase against Lord Dunmore, did not touch Virginia until 1780 (except for the burning of Portsmouth and fighting in the backcountry), supply was largely a Continental concern. The first deputy quartermaster general for the southern department was the same William

Finnie, appointed in 1776. In March 1780 General Washington directed that Richmond be one of four supply depots in Virginia for supplying the Continental army, particularly for flour, rum, hay, and corn; the other depots were Alexandria, Fredericksburg, and Petersburg.

During the early part of the war, local militia units secured supplies directly from local merchants. Most notably in Richmond and in Henrico County, Richard Adams, Thomas Prosser, and Turner Southall collected and sold supplies to the militia, for which they billed the government.

In summer 1780, the Congressional Board of War issued a directive that at least one deputy quartermaster general should reside in Richmond. Finnie, who still served as deputy quartermaster general in Richmond, had acquired a reputation for inefficiency. Moreover, he was caught in the middle of a dispute over reimbursement to the state by Congress for expenditures on the Continental army. Around November 1, Finnie apparently was relieved of his post as deputy quartermaster general in Virginia, was reassigned, or went on inactive duty.

From July to September 1780 several Continental officers collected supplies in Richmond for the Southern Army. Light-Horse Harry Lee gathered supplies for his cavalry battalion, and Lt. Col. Edward Carrington forwarded various equipment to "the Advanced Army." When General Greene passed through Richmond he found "The Quarter Master General's Department is totally deranged" in the state and "no Deputy appointed to act."

Greene instructed the new Continental commander in Virginia, General Steuben, to "get the Governor to make an Appointment without Loss of Time." Eventually Steuben himself appointed Maj. Richard Claiborne to be the deputy quartermaster general in Richmond, attached to Steuben's command. When the Continental quartermaster general, Timothy Pickering, approved the appointment, Claiborne entered his office in late 1780 as both deputy quartermaster general (Continental) in the state of Virginia and state quartermaster general.

Claiborne did the best he could in an impossible situation. As General Greene commented, Claiborne "succeeds in business as well as can be expected, where he is so much dependent upon a legislature who it is difficult to impress with the importance of giving aid timely as well as effectually." But Claiborne soon found his dual task too great, especially with the buildup of troops during the invasion period. He therefore resigned in March 1781 as quartermaster general for the state.

Capt. Henry Young, who arrived in Richmond from Edenton on March 31, took Claiborne's place as state quartermaster general. Within a week Young was so disheartened that he wanted to resign. But Colonel Davies got Steuben to persuade Young to stay on. Thus Claiborne handled the Continental quartermaster affairs, and Young, the state. With Claiborne absent part of the summer 1781, Young found that much of the Continental quartermaster "business devolves on me."

"I found nothing when I began," wrote Claiborne when he assumed office in January 1781. There was a great want of horses, forage, and wagons, and he did not know how to get them. In April he was just as frustrated.

The great demands which are made upon me for things to be furnished from this department [he wrote], both for the Southern Army, and the Troops within this State, alarm me more and more, as I have Not the means to answer any purpose whatsoever. I am called upon by the Commissary General of Purchases and the Commissary General of Military Stores for Wagons and horses daily, to transport their Stores, and have it not in my power to procure any. The preparations which the Baron [Steuben] directed me to make for the Cavalry and Infantry to be equipped in this State cannot be done, as I have not Money to purchase, and I cannot get Credit for an Article.

Immediately after Arnold's invasion of Richmond, horses could scarcely be found. To help move the "public stores" that "a few of the virtuous Inhabitants have collected" and also to obtain horses for Colonel Armand's corps then being outfitted, Claiborne ordered impressment of horses. But the officer he sent out came back with only five.

In May Claiborne still could not obtain horses even by impressment. As far as Richmonders were concerned, "none would undertake the matter for fear of getting the ill will of their neighbours, and I had no powers to compel them." Governor Jefferson conferred on Lafayette power to impress horses in counties "contiguous to the March of the Enemy," with payment in specie or paper. Because of the resistance of Virginians to impressment, the legislature at the end of 1780 voted that impressment had to be strictly by warrant and in time of actual invasion.

Stephen Southall, of the quartermaster's department, had to stand a court-martial in Richmond in December 1780 on the charge that he refused to supply General Weedon with forage for his horses. Weedon had offered to "advance his own money." Southall pleaded not guilty and testified that he had all he could do to supply General Steuben. He had neither the money or power of impressment, Southall said, otherwise he would have furnished the forage. He was acquitted by the thirteen-man court-martial, which had been convened by General Muhlenberg.

Providing food for the army was a responsibility shared by a commissary of supplies, commissary of purchases and issues, quartermaster general, commercial agent, state agents, victuallers, and local staff officers—all under the direction, as with other military affairs, of the state executive. Again there was the duplication of Continental and state functions.

Samuel Overton was designated a victualler of troops assembling in Richmond during the summer of 1776; John Syme provided food for those assembling at Hanover Town. John Mayo, Richard Adams, and William Cole procured flour, pork, and other provisions in 1776–77, most of it stored in Manchester "for the use of the Commonwealth." Richmond was one of seven places appointed to store provisions in October 1780 for counties along the James and Appomattox rivers.

In February 1782, "the Post at Richmond being in great want of provisions," Governor Harrison called upon "the virtuous Citizens" to appoint commissioners of the provision law to receive the "bacon Tax" and to deliver the bacon or pork they should collect to "the State commissary at the above Post."

During the first year of the war, militia commanding officers purchased clothes for members of their units and submitted the bills for reimbursement to the state. For making shoes, the state contracted leather out to the lowest bidder. William Aylett, as commissary of supplies in 1775, had charge of the Public Store in Williamsburg, which was later moved to Richmond. For the period 1779–81, both the clothier general, John Peyton, and the commissary of stores, William Armistead, at one time or another furnished clothing to state and regular troops.

An act of October 1780 required the counties to provide certain clothing. Henrico's quota amounted to 110 shirts, 55 overalls, 110 stockings, 55 caps, and 55 shoes. The county paid no heed to this requirement. Hanover County also failed to honor its quota; only Chesterfield made a very niggardly attempt to do so. Some of the leaders in Henrico County tried to do something to remedy this situation but failed in four sessions of the county court.

The shortage of clothes reached a crisis in December 1780. Continental troops being outfitted at Chesterfield Court House so that they could be sent to the Southern Army put a strain on the available resources. Militia that came and went also needed clothes, but seldom received any because the Continentals had first priority. Not only did new troops have to be supplied with clothing, but the Virginia regulars already with Greene's army were "literally naked" and therefore unfit for duty.

Richmond did not at once become a major depository for military stores. During 1775–76 Hanover Court House and Petersburg served as the chief magazines in central Virginia. In March 1777 the commissary of stores was directed to purchase gunpowder to be stored in the Henrico County and Dinwiddie County courthouses and in Chesterfield County under the care of Archibald Cary. A month later arms imported from the Dutch West Indies reached Richmond to be placed under the charge of the county lieutenant of Henrico County. In the same year Richard Adams and Turner Southall had the responsibility of receiving arms from the factory at Fredericksburg and supplying the Richmond and Henrico militia with them.

By 1779 Richmond had become the chief storage place in the state for powder, lead, cartridge paper, and other military stores. One half of the lead, mostly from the mines in Fincastle County, went to Richmond to meet the needs of the militia or to be sent to the Southern Army. In January 1781 Governor Jefferson directed the manager of the mines to send all the lead to Richmond.

As early as May 1777 plans were underway to build a

magazine in Richmond to serve as the central state depository for munitions and other military stores. Richard Adams and Turner Southall had charge of its construction. A notice in the *Virginia Gazette* advertised a meeting for interested workmen:

The subscribers being empowered to agree with workmen to build a GRAND PUBLICK MAGAZINE in the neighborhood of *Richmond, Henrico* county, which is to consist of two apartments, one a large wooden building, and the other to be of brick and stone, all carpenters, bricklayers and stone masons, willing to undertake the said work, are desired to give their attendance at Mr. *Gabriel Galt's* in the said town, on *Monday* the 23d of June, when a plan of the whole will be laid before the undertakers.

Nothing was heard further about this project, but Richmond may have had a magazine at a makeshift location before 1779.

Meanwhile, the state bought three and a half acres of land along the James River at Westham from John Ballandine to erect a state foundry. Iron, if not yet cannon, was being produced at the foundry by 1778.

Certainly Richmond had a magazine by late 1779. The Virginia Board of War ordered that "a house in a dry situation" be rented, until such time as a magazine could be built on land purchased by Richard Adams and Turner Southall of Fortunatus Sydnor "or elsewhere for the reception of the gun powder at Richmond Town." Some problem arose in getting a clear title to the land, but the magazine probably was located on the Sydnor property.

The state also established a "laboratory" in Richmond in 1779. The primary purpose of the laboratory was to repair arms and to make cartridges. The House of Delegates resolved that the governor and the Council should use "certain lots in the town of Richmond," which belonged to Ninian Minzies, a British subject, to erect several houses and a wooden shop for repairing arms. James Anderson, a blacksmith, took charge of the armorer's shop (repair shop), where he had the assistance of six state-owned slaves.

Capt. Lt. William Oliver superintended the state laboratory in 1780, but became sick in late August and requested to be allowed to go home. A Captain Scott "having come to town and being willing to take charge of the Laboratory" took over about September 1, 1780. Several months later Colonel Davies sent

Capt. Matthew Reid to Richmond "for the purpose of having the Arms and Stores received from the Militia, as they were discharged," returned to the state and of keeping them in good condition.

When the war moved to the South, the desirability of having a Continental laboratory in central Virginia became evident. Col. Timothy Pickering, a member of the Continental Board of War and already active in affairs of the quartermaster department, instructed General Gates to make whatever "temporary establishment" he could in Virginia. Pickering noted that "There is at Richmond already a small state laboratory, which perhaps you may be able to enlarge." During the summer of 1780, Colonel Carrington explored the possibilities of a laboratory. In agreement with the Virginia authorities, he decided that the Continental laboratory should be located at Westham.

Meanwhile, at the state laboratory in Richmond, musket cartridges were still being made and repair work done. In December James Anderson brought the whole state operation in arms repair and cartridge making to Westham. That involved no radical change, as the Richmond laboratory had already been engaged in repairing arms for the Southern Army, and, as Jefferson put it, "our militia have been long ago disfurnished of their arms for the use of the regulars." By mid-December the Continental-state laboratory at Westham was in full swing repairing muskets and manufacturing cartridges.

With the work at the remnant state laboratory in Richmond thus "impeded," the workers remaining there took over the guard duty. Ammunition left at the laboratory, cannon, and the shops had to be guarded.

It is, of course, an understatement to say that Arnold's invasion of early January 1781 disrupted the Continental-state laboratory. At both Westham and Richmond the enemy almost completely destroyed the equipment and the military stores. Afterwards, "proper workmen" could not be found, and artificers were "otherwise employed."

Some efforts were made to restore the Westham works. But throughout 1781 the authorities debated whether Westham—or even Richmond—was a proper place for the laboratory and military stores. They regarded both places as unsafe.

About all that was left of the Richmond magazine by mid-1781 were cannonballs and shells strewn about the town. Most military stores had been taken out of the enemy's reach to Albemarle Old Courthouse, Staunton, or Point of Fork. Lead and some cannon remained at Westham.

In December 1781, after Yorktown, "The Laboratory at Westham being now at a Stand," a guard of Captain Allen and his men were ordered to Richmond, where a magazine now served the town and the immediate area. Westham continued to experience difficulties. James Anderson reported in March 1782 that the artificers refused to work, because of insufficient provisions and because there was no house "at that place for their Reception."

In February 1783 the Virginia Executive appointed Capt. John Peyton, the former clothier general, "to take under your charge and direction the general Superintendance of the Military Stores, Arms, Ammunition &c." While Point of Fork would be "the grand repository of Military Stores," the Executive stipulated that 1,200 stands of arms be placed in Richmond "with the usual proportion of fixed Ammunition." Several months earlier, fifty stands of arms and ammunition had been given to the city of Richmond, and the Common Hall directed militia captains Robert Mitchell and John Brooke to distribute them "among the Citizens," taking receipts.

The records are scant on medical services during the early years of the war. But Richmond, especially after it became staff headquarters in 1780, figured prominently as a center for medical administration.

At the outset, various individuals in Richmond secured medical supplies and attended the sick. Gabriel Galt received £54 in June 1776 for "nursing and attend'e, prov's &c to two sick soldiers of Capt. Patterson's comp." In July the state reimbursed Dr. William Foushee for "sundry medicines" for the Ninth Virginia Regiment and similarly, Dr. John K. Reade, surgeon for the First Battalion of minutemen, who provided "Medicines and attendance on sundry minute Companies" at Manchester.

In June 1780 the Virginia Council of State ordered the quartermaster in Richmond "to hire a house properly situated" for a hospital or to "build one with logs for temporary use." It authorized Dr. Foushee to "hire a nurse occasionally, or if one can be got on moderate terms, a standing one." It told the commissary of stores to issue to Foushee upon application, "rice, hominy, molasses, sugar, vinagar, spirit, fresh meats and vegetables, and to provide a cow."

By mid-September a house was still not ready in Richmond to serve as a hospital, and Dr. Foushee had in supply only several of the "articles" he needed. Colonel Davies complained to Steuben in November 1780 that "the hospital will always be in distress" unless the medical department were "better arranged. . . ." The fact that officers in the Continental medical department had not been paid in at least two years did not help matters, either.

From Trenton in November, William Shippen, director general of all Continental hospitals, sent a Dr. Jackson to Virginia to "establish hospitals at or near Richmond or where the commanding officer there, may think most convenient to the Troops in Virginia." At the time of the invasion, a temporary hospital had been set up at Chesterfield Court House. With the advance of the British, however, the hospital and hospital stores were removed to Westham. Presumably the supplies destroyed by Simcoe at Westham included some hospital stores.

Confusion reigned during the invasion period. Medical supplies sent from the North were entirely appropriated by the Continental medical department in Virginia—"a double misfortune" because the state was "almost without every useful Medicine." The hospital accompanied the army. As Dr. Matthew Pope, a Virginia regimental surgeon, wrote, the "General Hospital which at this moment is at Allens Creek Church in Hanover where it may be tomorrow I know not as we keep moving with the Army."

Illness continued to plague the troops during the spring 1781. Soldiers of Maj. John Nelson's state regiment, in Richmond in April 1781, were "totally unfit for service from poverty, sore backs &c." Smallpox, which raged in Richmond during summer 1781, intensified the need for a "general Hospital." Dr. Pope observed that in the absence of such a hospital all the "miserable objects . . . seeking asylum" were "strolling about the Countrey." Pope kept on urging the Virginia government to establish a central hospital.

After Yorktown the numbers of military sick increased, especially those suffering from dysentery and smallpox. But at last there was something that barely passed for a military hospital in Richmond. Dr. Pope reported, in November 1781, that "A Temporary Log House has been attempted to be built" to receive the sick and wounded: "It remains unfinished to the present Hour and would be insufficient for the purpose it was intended," he wrote. "At present there are Ten Men confined in a small Room the roof of which leaks like a Riddle so that when it rains the sick may as well be out of doors."

The central military hospital consisted of the log cabin, an apothecary shop, and the medical supplies. From Richmond medicines were sent to "the several Posts." The Council of State requested Dr. Pope to stay on as "Surgeon and apothecary" of the state of Virginia, which included the charge of the Richmond hospital, with a salary of twenty shillings a day. Dr. Pope declined. In his stead, Dr. Foushee took the appointment.

Foushee was soon busy examining numerous "invalids." The hospital regularly had about a half dozen patients. Besides giving physical examinations, Foushee had to see that Colonel Dabney's troops were sent medicines and hospital stores.

Foushee's appointment as surgeon general and director of the hospital ended April 22, 1783. Presumably the military hospital in Richmond ceased to function about the same time.

British prisoners of war came to Richmond under confinement, on parole, or as prisoner defectors seeking a new life in America. But the town did not become a center for detention of prisoners. Like all Virginia communities it lacked the total resources needed for a prisoner-of-war camp. Richmonders also felt that to concentrate prisoners of war in one place, especially at or near the capital, might incur the danger of a prisoner uprising.

Prisoners of war usually passed through Richmond on their way to places of confinement at Winchester, Charlottesville, Chesterfield Court House, Hanover County, and elsewhere. Throughout the war, however, Richmonders had contact with the prisoner-of-war element and often were not very happy about it.

The first prisoners of war came to Richmond in February 1776. Numbering about twenty-five in all, the group included wounded soldiers of the British Fourteenth Regiment, captured at Great Bridge in December; seamen deserters, also taken at the time of the battle and the skirmishing afterwards; and tories. Several may have been from British landing parties that burned Norfolk in January 1776.

The prisoners were quartered in a house of Turner Southall, then county lieutenant of Henrico. Abraham Cowley provided food, fuel, "other Necessaries," and the guard. Meals must have been scanty for the prisoners, as Cowley received from the state only one shilling per day for victualling them. John McKeand furnished linens. These prisoners of war were kept in Richmond until June 1776, and were then sent elsewhere.

The largest contingent of prisoners of war in Virginia was Burgoyne's whole British army, which had surrendered at Saratoga. Largely because of the shortage of provisions where the prisoners were quartered in Massachusetts, Congress, in November 1778, ordered them to Virginia. Washington appointed Col. Theodorick Bland to superintend the march. John Harvie, a planter in Albemarle and Augusta counties and later to be one of Richmond's most prominent citizens, convinced the legislature to station the so-called Convention troops (British prisoners taken at Saratoga) on his lands near Charlottesville.

After a trek of 623 miles, the captive army arrived at Charlottesville in January 1779. About 4,100 Convention troops had started out from Massachusetts. An estimated 350 died, deserted, or were exchanged during the march. Thus, about 3,750—equally divided between British and German troops—arrived at Charlottesville.

While the prisoners of war were settling down at the Albemarle barracks provided for them, some of the officers and men continued to Richmond. They had "the purpose of receiving, sorting, transporting, and guarding the clothing and necessaries for the troops of convention, from that place to the barracks." The soldiers had to spend several days in Richmond, and found that they had to pay exorbitant prices; a bed and poor board cost, in German money, two talers.

The baggage that arrived was spoiled and much of it missing. This was a disaster for the Convention troops because many of them had gone two years without an issue of clothes. Most of the men and some officers were "absolutely barefoot"; like their American counterparts, they had little money to buy anything, since their pay had long been in arrears.

Although, according to the Saratoga Convention, officers and men were to be kept together, Congress allowed their separation—a policy intended to encourage desertion. Virginia did not interfere with this policy at first. Officers could reside within a one-hundred-mile radius of Charlottesville. General Phillips, who was later to lead an invasion of Virginia in April 1781, lived at Blenheim, the estate of Landon Carter; General Riedesel resided at Colle, Phillip Mazzei's modest house near Monticello. Other officers took up residence as far away as Richmond, Chesterfield County, and Staunton.

Jefferson entertained Phillips, Riedesel, and other prisoner officers at Monticello. Other prominent Virginians did the same. Several officers of the Convention army "lived some time" in Archibald Cary's "Neighbourhood." Thomas Mann Randolph, Sr., entertained British officers at his Tuckahoe plantation in Goochland County.

Lt. Thomas Anburey of the Convention army recorded that he himself stayed at Richmond "beyond my original intention" because of "the hospitality of the neighboring gentlemen, who would not let me leave them without visiting the whole circle."

In May 1779 Richmonders had a chance to see Virginia's most infamous prisoner of war, the "Hair-buyer General." Lieutenant Governor Henry Hamilton, commander of the garrison at Detroit, had been captured by George Rogers Clark at Vincennes. Hamilton and twenty-six other captives, under a twenty-three man guard, were en route to Williamsburg for confinement. On May 21 the prisoner-of-war party reached Goochland Court House, and stayed several days at Thomas Pleasants's house at Beaver Dam. To keep out of sight as much as possible, the party took a "bye road" to Richmond, thirteen miles out of the way and "not getting sight of people or dwellings for a long time."

Reaching the outskirts of Richmond about one in the morning, Hamilton recalled, "The Sentries would not suffer us to go into town, nor would they call to the guard so we lay on the ground till relief came." Next day they entered Richmond, where they spent four days. "Having passed our time disagreably at Richmond, from the prepossession of the people against us, and the curiosity to see how such a set of Infernals carryed themselves who had each been more bloodthirsty than Herod the Tetrarch, we were marched to Chesterfield, where we were kept under a jealous guard."

A few prisoners of war from the southern campaigns were brought overland to Virginia, some escaping on the way. Their destination being Winchester, few traveled by way of Richmond. Perhaps the largest group comprised eighty British prisoners taken at Cowpens. Archibald Cary's nephew delivered to Richmond in November 1780 a group of prisoners possibly being forwarded by the Southern Army. Lieutenant Mann, in Richmond, had charge of some prisoners of war "that came from below," which may have meant the southern theater; Jefferson considered provisioning them to be the responsibility of the Continental issuing commissary.

Four seamen taken at Charleston were sent successively to Wilmington, New Bern, and Halifax, and eventually to Richmond. At Richmond the four prisoners—Lieutenant N. Vernon, Quartermaster Thomas Embree, Volunteer S. Willet, and Storekeeper Joshua Hamilton—petitioned Governor Jefferson to be paroled to General Arnold because, as prisoners of war for over a year, they were "Moneyless and without Necessaries."

John Cabeen, captured by the Americans in the South in 1778, got a parole and went to Richmond, where he married and settled down as a shoemaker. At the time of the British invasion, he "rented a place in Newcastle." On a visit to Richmond to collect money that was owed him, Cabeen was arrested and carried before Col. William Davies "on Suspicion of being not a friend to America." He claimed status of a prisoner of war, but one who did not want to be exchanged. Without receiving any hearing, Cabeen was taken to Charlottesville and clamped into irons. He petitioned Governor Jefferson that he might be released so that he could go home and provide for his family. Cabeen professed that he intended "to be an Inhabitant of America, as long as I live."

Under American policy and practice, most British military prisoners usually had the freedom to move about in a restricted area. Thomas Hamilton, in one of his first acts as Richmond's new town major in April 1781, allowed "the Liberty of the Town" to nine prisoners of war. He soon found that other prisoners of war wanted "to experience the same Indulgence." In an inspection of the Richmond prison, Hamilton discovered two persons claiming to be prisoners of war, a Captain Carre and "one Davis," who were in irons, for what reason he could not ascertain.

During the spring of 1781 a few British soldiers and scouts were always being picked up. While General Phillips pondered whether or not to cross the James and attack Lafayette in Richmond, the militia captured eight British soldiers on the south side of the river and brought them into Richmond.

At Yorktown, the British surrendered 7,241 troops. Washington dispersed them in various directions. Some of the prisoners of war apparently were detained briefly in Richmond and were probably put up at the jail along with civilian "defectors" taken at Yorktown.

William Rose, the jailor, reported on November 1 that a Captain Faulkner had delivered forty-five prisoners to him by direction of Major Anderson. Rose said that the jail could not provide for more than one-half of them. The remainder would have to be put up "in the open yard, where they are exposed to the Inclemency of the weather, and that many of them must inevitably perish." He also needed a guard.

With no state troops in Richmond at the time, George Webb of the state council requested a sixteen-man militia guard from Henrico County, "until more effectual Means can be fallen on for the Safekeeping of such prisoners." Because the jail in Richmond was full, Thomas Hyde, a Yorktown prisoner of war, simply stayed at the hospital under a "guard." When his guard quit, the jailor, William Rose, allowed him "to go at large in the Town and to assist me at the Jail." Rather than go back to Yorktown for exchange, Hyde asked to stay in America and become a United States citizen. Whatever the final outcome of his case, Hyde got permission for the time being to "remain in the town as his disposition seems to be harmless." Indeed, Hyde's and Cabeen's common desire to adopt the new country as their own was shared by a great many prisoners of war, both British and German. An unknown number—probably in the thousands—managed in one way or another to become Americans as soon as they could.

CHAPTER SEVEN

Law and Society in Richmond

RICHMOND'S POPULATION, somewhere around six hundred in 1776, had passed the one thousand mark by 1782 and could have reached twelve hundred by the end of 1783. Under the best of circumstances such growth would have brought problems. As it was, the dislocation and unrest of wartime contributed to the increase in crime that disturbed Richmond's citizens.

Strategically located on the supply route south, Richmond was a convenient stop for soldiers and suppliers. The burgeoning city attracted merchants and craftsmen intent on bettering their fortunes as well as drifters and vagrants. Soldiers passing through, the war over or their time served, sometimes stopped to collect back pay and found in Richmond entertainment to their liking. Some soldiers were stationed in the city, including a garrison to guard the jail. The young sons of local citizens also returned from the war, perhaps bringing with them the influences of their worldly companions.

The many new faces in the area fostered an atmosphere in which "disorderly houses" and thievery thrived. Horse stealing was a major problem, but debtors figured most frequently in court cases. Of the 234 cases that came before the Richmond hustings court in 1782 and 1783, 120 dealt with the collection of debts.

Horse stealing reached serious proportions in the Richmond area during the Revolution. A horse, certainly one of a person's most valued possessions and one of the easiest to be stolen, provided in itself a ready means of escape. Many newspaper items and at least one act of the legislature reveal the seriousness of the problem. An advertisement in January 1775 warns of a wandering preacher who had stolen a horse at Warwick and headed for Richmond. In August two horses were stolen from Archibald Cary's estate, Ampthill, near Warwick. In the fall of 1776, the General Assembly increased the reward for apprehending horse thieves.

Nevertheless, the problem grew. In 1779 a group of Henrico County freeholders, in petitioning the House of Delegates, asserted their belief that "great combinations are formed through this country to accomplish that villaneous purpose with greater safety." Even city officials and clergymen had their horses taken. Mayor John Beckley advertised in September 1783 that his horse had either strayed or been stolen from the commons in Richmond. In October someone stole a horse from the pasture of the Reverend Miles Selden, Jr., near Richmond.

A crime of another sort, counterfeiting, had the potential of being equally devastating to Virginians. In 1783 Robert Price, a tobacco inspector at Byrd's warehouses, conspired with about a dozen citizens of Caroline County in counterfeiting and forging tobacco notes. They also counterfeited financier Robert Morris's promissory notes, which were circulating as currency. Attorney General Edmund Randolph pointed out that the involvement of an inspector with "this scheme of villainy" made it "more perilous."

The conspirators were apprehended when two "penitents" decided to give evidence against the others. The most notorious of the group, John Purcell, was tried before the general court in Richmond and was found guilty. His sentences totaled thirty-six months in jail, six days in the pillory, and £800. Purcell had served only a few months when he escaped from the public jail in Richmond and fled to North Carolina.

Randolph described Byrd's inspector of tobacco, Robert Price, as the "cornerstone of the villainy." He was charged before the Henrico County Court with "Forging, Counterfeiting and passing Inspectors Tobacco Notes knowing them to be so." After a trial, in which Price himself testified, the court stood divided, and Robert Price was acquitted. He resigned as an inspector soon thereafter.

The problem of forged tobacco notes on Richmond warehouses arose again in the latter part of 1783. The inspectors at Rocketts gave public notice that a forged tobacco note on that warehouse had surfaced; they feared others might be in circulation.

Arsonists burned part of the main structure of the Richmond ropewalk in 1783, as well as houses associated with it. A reward of five pounds was offered to the person revealing the culprits. Their conviction would increase the reward to fifty pounds.

Theft increased alarmingly in the Richmond area in 1782. Some citizens blamed the crime and disorder on slaves whose masters gave them too much freedom. A number of owners allowed their slaves to hire themselves out, returning to their masters the money they received. Others permitted their slaves to fend for themselves and pay their owners a regular sum.

Thirty-three leading citizens of Richmond and of Henrico County, petitioning the General Assembly in June 1782, expressed their concern that this practice contributed to the crime problem and to unrest among the slaves. A sympathetic legislature acted immediately to provide a remedy. The law enabled a citizen to have arrested slaves allowed to go at large and to hire themselves out. The local court could ultimately have such a slave sold.

Reflecting this concern about slaves having too much freedom, the Common Hall summoned prominent Richmonder and former Common Hall member Isaac Younghusband to appear before it in October 1782 because he had rented a house to two male slaves. In August 1783 the Common Hall received information that Dick, a slave belonging to William Armistead of New Kent, was going at large within the city as a freeman. Accordingly, the Common Hall ordered Dick to appear before it. Since Dick did not comply with the order, it can be assumed that he left town.

Attorney General Edmund Randolph, writing to James Madison in August of 1782, blamed the rampant crime on a gang of blacks and whites led by a "notorious" robber:

The laxness and inefficacy of government really alarms me. A notorious robber, who escaped from gaol about a twelvemonth ago, has associated in his villainies a formidable gang of blacks and whites, supposed to amount to fifty. They disperse themselves judiciously for the accomplishment of their work, and the elusion of punishment: and have perpetrated some of the most daring and horrid thefts. An attempt has been often made to arrest this prince of the banditti: but it has hitherto miscarried. Nay I do not believe, that government can by any means in its power effect the seizure of this man. I live in the center of the late depredations, and have no other hope to avoid their wickedness, than by the awe which my office may create.

About the same time that Randolph was writing Madison, the Common Hall of Richmond petitioned the governor about the same problem. The petition (see fig. 33) put the blame for

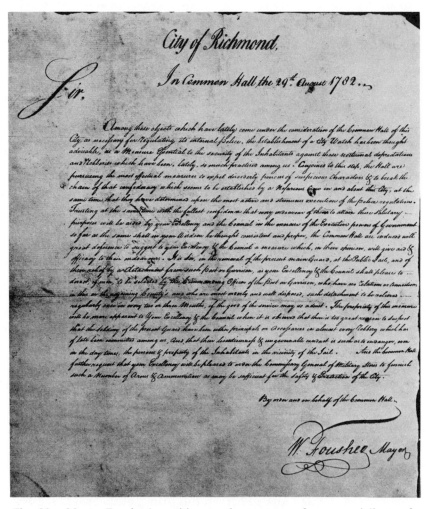

Fig. 33. Mayor Foushee's petition to the governor for a new jail guard. (Courtesy of the Virginia State Library.)

"those nocturnal depredations and Robberies which have been, lately, so much practised among us" on a "confederacy which seems to be established by a Nefarious Crew in and about this City." The petition stated further: ". . . there is too great reason to Suspect that the Soldiery of the present guard have been either principals or Accessories in almost every Robbery which has of late been committed among us, And that their licentiousness & ungovernable conduct is such as to endanger, even in the day time, the persons & property of the Inhabitants in the vicinity of the Jail."

The Common Hall requested that the main guard at the public jail be replaced with a garrison, "orderly and well disposed," whose members had no relations or connections in Henrico or the adjoining counties. And to prevent the recurrence of the problems, the new guard was to be relieved regularly once every two or three months. Complaints surfaced afterward from time to time about the disorderly behavior of guardsmen stationed within the city, but they were not again suspected of direct involvement in crime.

The Common Hall also appointed a sergeant and eventually four constables as law-enforcement officers. In addition, it employed four special watchmen. A watchman and a constable would form a patrol to be on duty in the city every night under a rotation system. In an effort to attract good men, the city exempted each constable and watchman from paying all city taxes.

This night watch was to take into custody any person on the streets after ten at night, and behaving in a riotous, disorderly, or suspicious manner. The following morning an alderman would decide whether to free the prisoner or to commit him to the workhouse for a maximum of twenty-four hours of hard labor. The firing of a gun, beating of a drum, sounding of a trumpet, or making of any other unusual noise was prohibited, with the fine doubled if the offense occurred at night.

Richmond's original charter gave the Common Hall authority to expel any disorderly person who had not been a resident in the city for twelve months. Putting teeth into this provision, the Common Hall now decreed that any would-be new resident must apply to the mayor, giving his name, profession, and last place of residence. The mayor could also require that the applicant put up security for good behavior during his residence. A person who failed to establish legal residence could be expelled.

Under this requirement, the Common Hall summoned fifty-seven men and twenty women who had not acquired legal residence or had other minor complaints against them between July 1782 and December 1783. Twenty-seven, including seven women, were required to put up security in order to stay in the city. Fifteen, of whom seven were women and two were men with families, had to leave the city.

Thirty persons, nineteen men and eleven women, were summoned before the Common Hall between July 1782 and December 1783 for keeping a "disorderly House" or a "riotous and disorderly house." Four of these, two women and two men, also faced a charge of retailing liquor without a license. Of those summoned, fifteen actually appeared. The Common Hall expelled from the city two persons, both women; required one woman and nine men to put up security that they would end the practices of which they were accused; and dismissed as groundless the charges against one woman and two men.

All accused law violators came before the Richmond hustings court after the city was incorporated in July 1782. The court heard cases involving both felonies and misdemeanors. However, it only had power to acquit in these cases. If, on examining the evidence, the court determined that the case should be tried, cases involving felonies were sent to the state General Court, and misdemeanors to the Henrico County Court.

Despite the complaints about crime, only ten criminal cases actually came before the Richmond hustings court during the period. In the only murder trial, in August 1782, George Todd, was found not guilty. The only theft case involved the examination of William Perry on the suspicion of breaking open the storehouse of James Roane and stealing goods worth £230. He too was acquitted.

Patrick Longan was examined for offering in payment a tobacco note he knew to be counterfeit. The court found Longan innocent of this felony. The only felony defendant not acquitted was William Cooke, charged with knowingly passing a forged military interest warrant. The hustings court sent Cooke's case to the General Court—which, ironically, acquitted him.

Three misdemeanor cases came before the Richmond hustings court during 1782–83. The court, divided in its opinion, dismissed one case. It found two defendants guilty of a misdemeanor and turned them over to the Henrico County Court for further action.

To handle criminal cases involving slaves accused of capital offenses, local courts in Virginia, after 1692, acted under commissions of oyer and terminer. Only three slaves came before the Richmond hustings court meeting as a court of oyer and terminer in 1782 and 1783. All were found guilty of grand larceny. Their punishment was immediate. They were first burned in the left hand in the presence of the court, and each was then tied to the end of a cart and led down Main Street, two with cow horns affixed to their foreheads. Following this humiliation, two received one hundred lashes and one received fifty lashes "well laid on" the bare back.

Like the hustings court, the Henrico County Court had few criminal cases. Only sixteen cases came before it between October 1781 and December 1783, the period for which court records are available. In four murder trials the court acquitted two defendants and sent two before the General Court. Of three men accused of horse stealing, two were sent before the General Court, and one was acquitted.

In the only case of burglary, Daniel Bridgwater and Samuel Thomas were charged with grand larceny for stealing a bag of salt. As no witnesses appeared to give testimony against them, they were acquitted. Philemon Williams was charged with "willfully shooting a loaded musket at William Mosby and maiming him." The court determined that Williams should be tried at the next General Court. Isham Allen was charged with "getting a Bastard Child upon a single woman," Martha Locket. However, the magistrate making the preliminary examination had failed to take Martha Locket's testimony in writing, so the case was dismissed on a technicality.

The Henrico County Court, meeting as a court of oyer and terminer, was more lenient to the four slaves it tried. It acquitted two; one had his crime reduced from a felony to a misdemeanor; and the fourth pleaded guilty to a felony and received a light sentence: to be burned in the left hand and receive fifteen lashes on his bare back.

The court periodically directed the sheriff to summon a grand jury of twenty-four freeholders to inquire of offenses generally. These general investigations of the grand jury usually dealt with minor lawbreaking and resulted in presentments being made to the court.

Henrico County grand juries offered a variety of presentments during the Revolution, the largest number against surveyors of roads for failing to do their jobs. One interesting presentment charged two justices of the peace, Col. John Pleasants and Isaac Younghusband, for "prophane swearing." Other presentments included "harboring a deserter," "keeping a tippling house," "retailing liquor," and "keeping a disorderly house."

In November 1782 a grand jury made presentments against fifty-eight people for failing to list their taxable property. The list included such prominent Richmonders as Samuel Ege and John McKeand. McKeand had been elected a member of the Common Hall, Richmond's governing body, the previous July.

Thirty-one people, referred from lower courts for criminal offenses other than treason, came before the General Court meeting in Richmond between December 1781 and December 1783. Fifteen appeared for horse stealing, three for murder, three for manslaughter, three for robbery, three for deceit (such as passing a counterfeit warrant), one for forgery and deceit, one for burglary, one for grand larceny, and one for rape. The court convicted and sentenced to be hanged all except five of those tried.

Most of the persons tried before the general court came from the lower economic classes. Of the thirty-one men who stood trial, the occupations of seventeen were given; eleven laborers, one carpenter, two wagon drivers, two soldiers, and one planter. No women were tried for criminal offenses before the hustings court, the Henrico County Court, or the General Court during this period.

Some citizens were concerned that the law required death sentences for persons found guilty of most felonies. A Richmond paper in 1782 carried the following comment.

A correspondent laments the number of capital punishments imposed by our present laws, and hopes that motives of humanity will conspire with those of true policy to induce the Legislature to adapt them more equally, and instead of depriving our fellow men of their lives for trifling offences, consign them to such laborious employments as will at once punish the criminal, promote useful public works, and present to the world living and striking instances of the vengeance due to crimes—our mines, our canals and gallies, are very proper places for the employement of such criminals.

In a report to Governor Harrison in 1783, the General Court judges who convicted five men for horse stealing commented: "We cannot but lament that the laws relating to capital punishments are in many cases too severe."

On the other hand, stiffer penalties also had proponents. Citizens of Richmond and Henrico County in a petition to the House of Delegates in 1779 complained that "horse stealing has become so common from an idea that no crime ought to be punished with death but murder, and from the lenity heretofore shown to malefactors in general, your petitioners' property is entirely insecure. . . ."

In actual fact, seventeen of the twenty-six convicted criminals sentenced to death by the General Court between December 1781 and December 1783 did receive pardons. Ten of the fifteen convicted of horse stealing, two of the three convicted of robbery, but none of the three convicted of murder got pardons. Of the seventeen pardons, five were given on condition that the recipient serve in the army. Other conditions attached to the pardons specified one to seven years of work at the public laboratory or the lead mines. A youth twelve years old and eight others received unconditional pardons.

The Henrico County Jail, which also served the city of Richmond, became the public jail of the state of Virginia when the capital was moved in 1780. Prisoners awaiting trial by the General Court and those sentenced by the General Court were kept in the jail. The keeper, William Rose, attended the General Court and carried out its orders. In 1783 the Reverend Mr. Blackgrove, already attending the prisoners in jail and at executions, joined the official staff to continue this function on the state payroll.

The Henrico County Jail, built in 1752, occupied the

southwest corner of Twenty-Second and Main streets. A pair of stocks and a pillory stood nearby. The gallows waited in Shockoe Valley, just north of Broad Street, near the point where Fifteenth Street would cross Broad if it were extended. The condemned man rode from the jail to the gallows on a cart, accompanied by a clergyman. After allowing the convicted criminal his last words, the sheriff of Henrico, serving as hangman, would place the rope around his neck and the offender would be "turn'd off" the cart.

Crowds gathered to watch the executions. The *Virginia Gazette* of November 30, 1782, reported such an execution and a dramatic last-minute pardon: "Yesterday was executed at the Gallows near this city pursuant to his sentence, Maurice Wheeler, from Lancaster County, for murder. . . . four, for horse stealing, were conditionally pardoned" under the gallows, to serve in the continental army during the war.

Converting the small county jail into service as a public jail for the state brought immediate problems. The jail's two small rooms, ten feet square, were often crowded, with sometimes as many as eleven prisoners in one room. A committee reporting to the General Court on its investigation of the jail in 1781 declared it "very insufficient for the number of Prisoners contained therein. . . ." They reported finding "no conveniences for the use of the prisoners and Observe that the Gaoler has kept it much cleaner than was expected," but despite his endeavours it was still "unwholesome and inconvenient" for the prisoners.

Plans for establishing the capital in Richmond had included the enlargement of the Henrico County Jail. The Directors of Public Buildings contracted with Drury Wood and Barret Price to enlarge the jail. But Wood and Price ran into constant problems. The army confiscated building materials they had gathered and also recruited their only waggoner and some of their workers. Several of their Negro workmen left with the British during Arnold's invasion. Wood and Price never could carry out the planned enlargement.

Because of the crowded conditions and the danger of spreading infectious diseases, the General Assembly in 1781 recommended that a temporary building be rented for housing some of the prisoners. No evidence shows that this was ever done. Finally, in 1783 the state built a new public jail near the old one, and gave Henrico County the right to use it in return for giving up the old jail. The bricks, timber, and nails from the old prison were to be used by the state to build a jail keeper's house on the same site.

Houses had been rented for Rose from Richard Adams and Samuel Ege, but they were too far away for the jailer to keep order in the prison and to prevent escapes. Compounding the problem, Rose wrote the General Court in 1783, "the Prison being surrounded by Tipling Houses, Liquor is conveyed to them by the Guards and disorderly People, who are continually plying round the pickets. They drink frequently to excess, and immediately the Prison is all riot. . . ." Several times Rose had felt his life endangered while attempting to quell the rioters.

Rose, who had an interesting penal philosophy, believed he could prevent such problems if he lived at or near the prison. A jailer's house built on the site of the old jail would also help by blocking the prison from the view of the people passing up and down the street. "Prisoners, highly criminal, should be carefully, and constantly attended to, and taught both to fear, and love their keeper," he wrote to the General Court. "Those affections constitute his and their Safety. To accomplish these ends it is absolutely as necessary that the Keeper should live close to, or under the same roof with his prisoners, as that a school Master should reside in the same room with his Scholars."

Supplying labor to cook, wash, and attend the prisoners was a constant problem. The fact that the jail yard lacked a pump increased the labor, for a large amount of water was needed for drinking, washing, cleaning, scouring, and cooking. The most time-consuming and unpleasant task was "carrying the Buckets of Excrement and urine upon the Head to the River three or four Times a Day. . . ."

Rose needed at least two people at all times to do this work, and he used both hired slaves and public slaves. The hired slaves would often run away "so filthy and laborious was their employment." The public slaves usually worked harder, but even they ran away occasionally. And during the invasion the various departments of the army reclaimed the slaves that Rose had on hand.

The army guard for the public jail, a nagging problem for the city of Richmond, was also one of Rose's major sources of complaint. He wrote the governor in July 1783: "From the long experience I have had of Prison Guards, . . .I have found them rather an expensive nuisance than any real security to me, or to the Public." Rose felt a brick wall built around the new jail "would equally secure the criminals without a Guard." Though he got the brick wall, the prison guard was also retained. Rose later wrote again to the governor, requesting that the guard be removed and pointed out that he did not know of a single instance where the guard had prevented an escape but that he knew of several in which they had had a helping hand.

Besides criminals, the public jail in Richmond contained runaway slaves and debtors. The new jail provided separate quarters for debtors on the second floor. However, the builder had failed to include a second-floor fireplace, and in the fall of 1783 Rose felt the debtors were receiving a punishment "far beyond the intention of the Law or the wishes of the most sanguinary Creditors." A fireplace was added to alleviate their suffering.

To make life more bearable for the debtors, "prison bounds"—laid off in January 1783,—included ten acres around the jail, Tankard's Ordinary, and a passage six feet wide up the hill to St. John's Church. Henrico Sheriff Thomas Prosser, nevertheless, complained on behalf of debtors that the prison bounds included no "proper Houses of entertainment within the said bounds for persons in their situation." The Henrico County Court appointed a new committee to draw up new bounds that "to them shall appear most likely to remove such inconvenience."

It would be logical that some runaway slaves would go to a growing town like Richmond, where they might attempt to pass themselves off as free blacks or as slaves permitted to hire themselves out. However, local records reveal only one definite reference to runaways being in Richmond. William Rose wrote in July 1783 of the public jail being crowded with sixteen prisoners, including "Criminals, Debtors, and Runaways."

About the same time, Gilley Jackson, described as an "itinerant resident," was required to appear before Common Hall because doubt rose as to whether she was bond or free.

The Common Hall gave her a month to produce a proper certificate of her freedom. Other new blacks appeared in the city in 1783. The Common Hall summoned Pharis Dunkenfield to appear for failing to acquire a legal residence and Thomas Pore for displaying "disorderly and abusive conduct."

Scattered reports of runaways from the Richmond area during the war years can be found in surviving records. Three Henrico County residents, Lewis Ball, Fortunatus Sydnor, and John Hales, advertised during 1775 for slaves that had run away. Dr. Robert Brown of Richmond lost a fourteen-year-old boy who ran away from him while in Norfolk. Five public slaves ran away from the Westham foundry in 1777. Two ran away from the Richmond ropewalk. One was a boy and the other a thirty-year-old man named Amos, described as possessing an "incorrigible disposition to villany, having his back much marked by whipping."

Life for blacks in Richmond during the Revolution included special regulations. A slave could not be on the street after ten o'clock at night without written permission from his owner. Blacks, slave or free, could not hold nightly meetings except at Christmas and on other special occasions. Even then slaves had to have written permission from their masters or mistresses.

The city forbade Negroes, both slave and free, to play cards, roll dice, play ball, or play any other game for money or other items. No black was to take part in or even attend any cockfight or horse race. Blacks were not to commit any breach of the Sabbath by playing any of the above-mentioned games on that day, though not for money.

A black could receive up to thirty lashes for any of the above offenses. Any person convicted of gambling with a slave or of playing any game with him on the Sabbath was to be fined twenty-four shillings, and if he could not pay, he was to receive twenty lashes. Violation of regulations that applied to both slaves and free, white and black, usually incurred a fine unless the person was a slave, or unless he could not pay the fine. Then the penalty prescribed was a certain number of lashes.

Slaves could bring their own provisions to sell in the public market only on Saturday afternoons and Sundays. Even then, a slave had to have written permission from his owner, specifying the articles that he could bring to market. The items could be exposed for sale before sunset on Saturday afternoon and before ten o'clock on Sunday. If not sold by those times, the provisions had to be removed from the city.

Under the social system of the time, free blacks and slaves occupied much the same position. Free blacks met and mingled with the slaves "on a plane of almost perfect social equality." Out of this relationship often came marriage. For example, a free black, Benjamin Bilberry, married Kate, the slave of Abraham Cowley.

Intermarriage between whites and blacks, whether slave or free, was illegal. The Common Hall summoned Sarah West in 1783 on the charge that she was cohabiting with a slave and that she had failed to acquire a legal residence. When she acknowledged the charges, the Common Hall ordered her to leave town within fifteen days or be jailed. Whites were forbidden to entertain blacks in the taverns or ordinaries. John Lockley, a tavern keeper at Rocketts, had his license suspended for a month for keeping a "very disorderly house" and entertaining and retailing liquor to blacks.

Contrary to the impression that might be gained from various petitions of the time, crime was not widespread among the free blacks of Richmond. No free black was prosecuted for a crime in Richmond or in Henrico County during the war years for which records are available. The most serious complaints charged James Anderson and Kate Burcher with keeping a "disorderly house." Peter Robertson, listed as Kate's husband in the 1782 tax list, was a slave belonging to Isaac Armistead on hire to Kate. After charges were brought against Kate, the Common Hall ordered Armistead to "discharge the hire aforesaid and dispose of the said Negro Peter in some other manner." However, Kate did not change her ways and in less than four months she again appeared before the Common Hall for keeping a disorderly house.

At special courts of oyer and terminer for the trial of slaves, witnesses for and against the accused could be heard, and he was allowed to speak for himself. Blacks could be witnesses in this court, but even free blacks were not allowed to testify against whites in any court. Owners could appear in defense of their slaves. Trials were held without a jury, the judges of the court deciding the case. A divided vote of the justices constituted an acquittal. If a slave received a death sentence, a request for pardon could be made to the governor, but if no pardon was given and the slave was executed, the state reimbursed the owner the value of the slave.

The courts of Richmond and Henrico County sentenced no slaves to capital punishment from October 1781 to December 1783, the period for which records are available. Those found guilty of felonies or of misdemeanors got physical punishment and public humiliation instead. The Henrico County Court had a higher acquittal rate for accused slaves than for the white persons it tried. The Richmond hustings court, on the other hand, had a much higher conviction rate in its slave cases and imposed stiffer penalties on those convicted. This may reflect greater fear of a slave crime problem in the city, where blacks formed a large proportion of the population and whites felt a greater need for control. No slaves were tried for crimes in either Richmond or Henrico County in 1783.

Manchester, Virginia's leading slave market in the colonial period, continued in that role during the first part of the Revolution. An advertisement appearing in the *Virginia Gazette* in January 1775 offered for sale at Manchester "Thirty valuable Virginia-born slaves, consisting of men, women and children." Another advertisement, in January of the next year, listed one hundred Virginia-born slaves for sale at Manchester, among them some female house servants, a carpenter, and a shoemaker. In October 1776 fifty Virginia-born slaves, including house servants and a carpenter, were offered for sale.

After 1776 the slave market in the area shrank and moved to Richmond, usually in front of one of the local taverns on Henrico County court day. In November 1777 a number of slaves were sold in front of Galt's Tavern, and six slave women were advertised for sale there in February 1778. Slaves seem to have been scarce during these years, as both the state of Virginia and Richmonder David Ross had trouble purchasing enough to meet their needs. With the ending of the war, the state's needs dropped to the point where it sold some of its slaves in Richmond.

By 1778 many white Virginians shared the humanitarian view that slavery was wrong. Others feared that they might be overwhelmed by the black population. Therefore, Virginia passed a law forbidding anyone from bringing more slaves into the state. A violation would result in a fine of £1,000 and the freeing of the slave.

Some citizens supported a movement to emancipate the slaves. But until 1782 a slaveowner could not free one of his own slaves. The General Assembly had to pass an act for the manumission of the individual slave. An interesting request for a manumission came from Richmonder Benjamin Bilberry in 1780. His wife Kate had been the property of Abraham Cowley. With a lot and house Bilberry had acquired on Shockoe Hill, he purchased his wife from Cowley. He was then shocked to learn that instead of being liberated from slavery, she had just changed masters: at his death she, with her future offspring, would be subject to slavery again. Bilberry was especially irked to know that by the law of the commonwealth he was forced to hold his own wife in a "slavish bondage without the power of making her as free as himself."

The General Assembly did emancipate Kate. The record does not say what happened to Benjamin Bilberry. But in his will dated 1785 Robert Baine freed James Bilberry, mulatto son of Kate Bilberry, living with him as a slave. Baine also willed that Kate, who was then attending him, "enjoy the use, benefit and possession" of his dwelling house in Richmond, including kitchen and garden for twelve months after his death.

The principles of the Revolution, such as natural equality and individual liberty, influenced many people in Virginia to see slavery in a new light. In the Richmond area, Quakers especially desired to free their slaves. Believing that freedom is the natural right of all mankind, Quakers petitioned the House of Delegates in 1780 for permission to legally manumit their slaves. They had already prohibited their members from purchasing slaves. In his will of 1779 Richmond Quaker Joshua Storrs left his slaves to some of his fellow Quakers to provide them as much liberty as possible. The Henrico County Court in 1782, tried two Quakers, Samuel Parsons and Robert Pleasants, for letting their slaves go at large as freemen. Parsons was acquitted, but Pleasants was found guilty and fined ten pounds.

The General Assembly acted favorably on the Quakers' petition in 1782. Under a law passed in that year, a person could emancipate the slaves he owned through his will or some other written document or by declaring his intent in court. As a protection for the freed slaves, the person liberating the slaves or his estate was required to support and maintain any slave not of sound mind and body, any over forty-five, and any male under twenty-one or female under eighteen. With the passage of this law, prominent area Quakers began immediately freeing their slaves. Samuel Parsons freed nine, William Binford freed eighteen, and Robert Pleasants freed seventy-eight.

Finally, two laws passed in 1783 enhanced the position of some blacks in Virginia. One extended freedom to any slave who had substituted for a free person in the army. The other defined "citizen" to include all free persons, black or white, born in the state.

CHAPTER EIGHT

A Mercantile Town

THE PERIOD of the Revolution brought significant changes in Richmond's economy. From a small-town center for trading raw materials, the city and its immediate area branched out into other economic endeavors. The demands of the war and the loss of supplies from Europe, as well as Richmond's new political importance as the capital of the state, gave impetus to the growth. Trade in raw materials and agricultural products increased, and manufacturing, mining, and crafts took their places in the economic picture as well.

Richmond had come into existence as a trading center and had served that function for the Indians even before the English colonization. Located at the falls of the James, the town provided easy access for inland farmers to the ocean-going ships that came up the river to Richmond. Planters brought tobacco (their main crop), and other products, such as corn, wheat, and flour, down the James River and by land to be traded for goods from England. Richmond's strategic location for trade made it attractive as a site for the capital.

English merchants dominated this trade until 1750, when Scottish trading companies became predominant in Virginia. The Scottish merchants had agents in Virginia, known as factors. These factors centered their activities—and some settled permanently—in towns such as Richmond, located on navigable rivers. They usually built warehouses to store their goods.

As the Revolution approached, some of the foreign-born merchants in Richmond swore allegiance to the patriot cause and stayed on. One such Scottish merchant and ship owner, James Buchanan, became a member of Richmond's first Common Hall and one of the Directors of Public Buildings. He had come to Richmond at age twenty in 1757. Another was Common Councilman John McKeand, who came to Richmond at age twenty in 1762.

Revolutionary pressure eventually forced all merchants of

Great Britain to leave the country unless they had shown friendship for the American cause or had wives and children in America. When the capital was moved to Richmond, the state government confiscated the property of loyalist merchants in the city for its own use.

The 1782 tax census of Richmond listed the occupations of 147 persons. Of these, thirty-three—or 22 percent—were merchants, among them: Richard Adams, William Armistead, Isaac Younghusband, Isaiah Isaacs, Jacob Cohen, John McKeand, James Buchanan, George Nicholson, William Pennock, William Hay, Benjamin Harrison, Jr., Henry Banks, James Hunter, and Alexander Nelson.

Trading companies operating in Richmond during the Revolution included Hunter, Banks, and Company; Nelson, Heron, and Company; William Pennock and Company; Benjamin Harrison, Jr., and Company; Joshua Storrs, Hugh Walker, and Company; David Ross and Company; Stewart and Hopkins; and Cox and Higgins. These companies carried goods in and out of Richmond, trading with the Caribbean area and with Europe. Some of the companies or individual merchants licensed their ships as privateers to make war on British commerce as well as to carry on trade.

Despite England's attempt to prevent it, trade in and out of Richmond continued during the Revolution. In August 1776 a permit was issued to the schooner *Bettsy* to sail to Hispaniola with a cargo of tobacco, corn, and flour. In December the schooner *Good Intent* slipped through the British blockade to arrive in Richmond around Christmas. The cargo of the *Good Intent* included gunpowder, nails, osnaburgs, white linen, men's and women's white silk hose, needles, pins, writing paper, rum, and molasses. In April 1777 arms reached Richmond from the Dutch island of Saint Eustatius in the Caribbean aboard the boat *Molly.*

A large amount of tobacco was still being exported to Europe and the West Indies in 1777, thus allowing Virginia to maintain her credit in neutral countries. In an effort to prevent this export of tobacco, the British usually burned all the warehouses they could reach. In February 1779 the warehouses at Richmond were crowded with tobacco. English privateers threatened to capture any ship that dared to leave port.

Nevertheless, a few small boats reached Bermuda, and their owners were the only merchants in Richmond who had commodities in their stores.

The British blockade tightened early in 1781. Although ships in trade continued to make their ways in and out of Richmond, their owners often suffered heavy losses. Commercial vessels suffered not only the ravages of the British navy but the additional hazard of being impressed by the state for military service.

Trade in and out of Richmond intricately involved the system of state tobacco warehouses and "inspections," and the landings associated with them. The General Assembly at its October 1776 session had reestablished the earlier system of public warehouses "for the reception and inspection of tobacco at or near the heads of the rivers and creeks." It included the Byrd and Shockoe warehouses in Richmond and the Rocky Ridge warehouse across the river at Manchester.

The county courts exercised ultimate authority over the warehouses and the inspection system. The court appointed two of its members to examine and adjust the scales at each warehouse. From a list of men proposed by the court, the governor chose two inspectors and one assistant for each location.

Planters usually brought their tobacco in wooden casks known as hogsheads, each weighing about one thousand pounds. (See fig. 34.) The inspectors could approve only tobacco that they found to be "sound, well conditioned, merchantable, and clear of trash." Having done so, they stamped the owner's mark, a number, and the weight on the hogshead and gave the owner a note or receipt describing the kind of tobacco deposited.

The owner paid a fee for having his tobacco inspected and stored. From this money the warehouse company received its rent and the inspectors their salaries. If fees fell short, the inspectors got only what remained after other expenses were paid. They could not trade in tobacco themselves or receive any gratuity other than their salary. Neither could any inspector run for public office while serving as inspector. Informers of any violations were promised a large reward.

"Byrd's inspection" consisted of two warehouses. The older

Fig. 34.   Methods of bringing tobacco to the warehouses in Richmond. This engraving portrays transportation to market by two double canoes, by boat, by wagon and four-horse team, and by rolling a hogshead. (Courtesy of the Virginia State Library.)

Byrd warehouse occupied the block that is today bounded by Main, Fourteenth, Cary, and Fifteenth streets. A second warehouse stood on higher ground, at approximately the intersection of Fourteenth and Franklin streets. The Shockoe inspection also operated two warehouses in the same area: one was on the block formed today by Cary, Twelfth, Canal, and Thirteenth streets; the other covered the area where Fourteenth and Canal streets come together.

The Byrd and Shockoe warehouses used the Shockoe landing on the James River between what is today Fifteenth and Seventeenth streets. Shockoe landing was also known as the "Old Rock landing" because of a broad, flat rock located at the landing. The name "Shockoe" may come from the Indian word for stone—"Shacquonocan," as Capt. John Smith recorded it.

By 1780 ships were having difficulty getting to the Shockoe landing. Floods and an alteration in the course of Shockoe Creek where it entered the James River had caused large sandbars to form. These sandbars threatened complete blockage of the channel unless they were removed. Some citizens of Richmond declared themselves willing to provide money to turn Shockoe Creek into its old channel or to clear the channel to the landing. The General Assembly therefore granted the Directors of Public Buildings authority to take subscriptions for that purpose. Almost enough money had been raised to carry out the project when the British invaded the area and put an end to the scheme.

Since this navigation problem continued unsolved, some of the merchants, traders, and inhabitants of Richmond petitioned the House of Delegates on December 10, 1781, to establish a warehouse for the inspection of tobacco about a mile downstream from Shockoe landing at Rocketts landing. Rocketts landing—just upriver from where Gillies Creek flows into the James today, in the area that is now Fulton—got its name from Robert Rocketts, who had a ferry in that area as early as 1730.

The petitioners gave several reasons why a tobacco inspection near Rocketts landing would be of "great advantage to the trade" of Richmond. The owners of the land there had built a "large and commodious wharf to which vessels of considerable burthen may come. . . ." The proposed site of the inspection warehouse was so convenient to the landing that as many as fifty hogsheads per day could be loaded on board a vessel for half the expense required at Shockoe landing. Rolling the tobacco a considerable distance could be avoided and labor expense would be less.

A group of Shockoe area merchants quickly reacted to the Rocketts proposal. Presenting their own petition to the House of Delegates the following day, they pointed out that, before sand clogged the channel of the river, ships involved in both internal and foreign trade used the Shockoe landing, whereas "vessels fit for foreign commerce never used to land at Rocketts...." "Skillful engineers" believed the navigation problem could be solved at small expense by changing the course of Shockoe Creek and removing the sand. The petitioners therefore recommended that course as less expensive than building new warehouses at Rocketts.

The Shockoe petitioners also observed that a planned canal to connect the backcountry to Richmond "would be defective unless the navigation below the town was maintained...." Moving the tobacco inspection warehouses to Rocketts would take away the incentive to maintain navigation to Shockoe. People who had built stores and warehouses near the tobacco inspections would be hurt, and planters bringing their tobacco by water would be subject to "a fifth more land carriage." Some might carry their tobacco from Westham to Manchester. Therefore, the petitioners asked that the tobacco inspection warehouses be kept where they were.

The House of Delegates rejected the Shockoe petition and decided to establish an inspection of tobacco on the land of Charles Lewis near Rocketts landing. Lewis agreed to build a warehouse for that purpose on lot no. 170, just downriver from where Peach Street intersects Dock Street today. The Shockoe and Byrd inspections were retained, thus increasing the inspections in or near Richmond to three.

Not only did the Shockoe inspection face new competition from the Rocketts inspection, but its warehouses, burned by the British in 1781, had to be rebuilt. Henderson, McCaul, and Company of Glasgow had owned the buildings, with one of the partners, James Lyle, as manager in Richmond. When Lyle refused to rebuild the warehouses, the Henrico County Court

had them rebuilt by Drury Wood in 1782. Because of the need
for more space, additional buildings were erected at the
Shockoe site in 1783.

The Rocketts inspection also had more tobacco than it could
store in 1783, and the Henrico County Court had the storage
facilities there enlarged when Charles Lewis refused to enlarge
the warehouse himself. The fact that the owners refused to
rebuild or enlarge their warehouses being used for inspection
purposes suggests that the state was behind in its payments for
their use (as it was in many other obligations), or that the fee
received was insufficient to be profitable.

The British destroyed tobacco at Byrd's inspection, but seem-
ingly no warehouses were burned. Henrico County Court
records do not mention a need to rebuild warehouses after the
British occupied Richmond or to add storage space in 1783 at
Byrd's inspection as was necessary at Rocketts and Shockoe.

General Phillips burned the tobacco warehouses at
Manchester, across the river from Richmond, in April 1781.
Merchants in Manchester petitioned the House of Delegates to
restore them in order to avoid a loss of trade. Because re-
construction would require time, the General Assembly appointed James Lyle, David Patterson, and Francis Goode,
commissioners, to rent a house or houses for the immediate reception of tobacco.

Companies involved in the tobacco trade were the largest re-
tailers of goods imported into Richmond. No division between
wholesale and retail operations seems to have existed. Rather,
merchants offered their goods to any willing buyer at the established price. Among importers who also maintained "stores"
in Richmond, Henry Banks, James Hunter, Alexander Nelson,
David Ross, Isaiah Isaacs, Jacob Cohen, William Pennock, Isaac
Younghusband, and Benjamin Harrison, Jr. advertised in the
Virginia Gazette during the period 1776–83. In addition, Miles
Taylor placed an advertisement in February 1776 for "garden
and other seeds, lately imported from Italy," available at his
store. Another store was operated by Robert Mitchell.

During the revolutionary period Richmond's stores—rather
than being specialty shops—sold a wide variety of merchandise.
The British prisoner of war Thomas Anburey, who visited
Richmond in 1779, gave an interesting account of what the

stores were like. The town lacked "various branches of manu-
factures, such as linen-drapers, mercers, grocers, hosiers,
haberdashers, stationers, etc.," he wrote, "but all are comprized
under the name of merchant and store-keeper; and what are
called shops in England, are here denominated stores, which
furnish every article in life, not only necessary but ornamental,
and even jewelery. . . ."

The advertisements of the period confirm Anburey's
observation. Nelson advertised goods at the "Brick Store,"
including West Indian rum in hogsheads, muscovado sugar in
barrels, the best Madeira wine in pipes, alum salt, bar iron and
castings, sail duck, and a "general assortment of dry goods."
Isaacs, Cohen, and Company advertised "Dry and Wet Goods
and a parcel of Medecines." Miles Taylor's variety of seed
ranged from cabbage to wheat and included asparagus, broc-
coli, sweet basil, watermelon, and "horse beans." William Pennock offered for sale cloth, blankets, hose, gloves, needles, tin
wire, small anchors, French brandy, lemons, and paper.
Benjamin Harrison, Jr., included in his list of wares Queen's
china and copperware. Younghusband's store boasted the "best
French Hair Powder, in pound papers." Hutchins's map of the
"Kentucky Country" with a pamphlet describing the quality of
the soil was the special prize offered by Pennock's and Banks's
stores.

By 1783 specialty shops began to develop in Richmond. The
French Store, operated by Richard Gernon, limited its offerings to "dry goods." Thomas Brend, bookbinder and stationer,
had a shop adjoining Tankard's Tavern near the courthouse.
He advertised account and record books ruled in any direction,
"books fit for music," Bibles, Testaments, spelling books,
Starke's Virginia Justice, British quills, wafers, sealing wax, black
and red ink powder, and writing paper. Mons. Curot's leather
shop advertised sides of harness leather, foal and upper
leather, kipskins of black leather for couch covering, black
leather for bridle reins, leather for horse collars, blind bridles,
sets of gear for wagon horses, bridle bits, and buckles.

Very early in the city's life, the Common Hall responded to a
need for a regulated public market and slaughterhouse. They
felt that a central market would assure equal opportunity to all
citizens in obtaining food and supplies and would also

guarantee quality and wholesomeness of the food offered for sale in the city. A significant improvement in aesthetics would result, too, from confining sales and slaughter—with the resultant debris—to a single place, thus eliminating hawking on the streets. The central market would also be more convenient to the farmers.

An ordinance passed July 19, 1782, designated the market house on the city commons as "The Market of the City of Richmond," probably located where it is today, at the corner of Seventeenth Street and Main. The ordinance set aside Wednesdays and Saturdays as "grand market days." On these days all items brought into the city for sale had to be brought first to the marketplace and had to remain there until twelve noon, or until sold. Fruit and fish, however, because of their perishable nature, could be removed from the market after two hours and sold at large.

Robert Rawlings, appointed the first "clerk of the market" under the ordinance, had broad duties. They ranged from maintaining cleanliness in the market to settling disputes between customers and sellers. The clerk was to examine all provisions brought to the market, to seize any he suspected of being unwholesome, and to adjust weights and measures.

The July 19 ordinance also dealt with meat offered for sale at the market. Meat could be brought into the city ready for sale. However, all animals brought live into the city were to be slaughtered only by the public butcher, appointed and licensed by the Common Hall.

Until a "proper" slaughterhouse could be erected, the butcher would function at a place, to be designated, that would be "least offensive to the Inhabitants, and not contiguous to the market." He should receive five shillings for each cow, one shilling six pence for each calf, and one shilling three pence for each lamb or sheep slaughtered. The absence of any butchering fee for pork suggests that perhaps only cured pork was offered in the market. Any person who failed to use the services of the butcher, as required, had to pay the fee anyway.

The city had considerable difficulty in staffing the position of public butcher. Joseph Daily, the first candidate, turned the job down. James Hughes took the job but soon after was found to be purchasing goods on the way to the market then reselling them at a higher price. (At about the same time—as will appear in later pages—he was arrested for treason.) Tanus Tate replaced Hughes as butcher in November 1782, but by the following May the Common Hall, having heard complaints of misconduct and a shortage of provisions at the market, was again looking for a butcher.

In an effort to encourage quality in the meat brought to market, the Common Hall established cash incentives for the persons bringing in the greatest quantity of the best quality meat in several categories. For instance, stalled beef received a higher reward than grass-fed beef, mutton slightly less than beef, and veal just under mutton.

Farmers in the Richmond area during the period of the Revolution experienced two of the traditional problems of farmers: plant disease and adverse weather conditions. Richard Adams wrote from Richmond in 1778 that there was a good prospect for all crops "except Wheat, which is much hurt with the rust." This and other problems prompted Governor Jefferson to write John Jay, president of the Continental Congress, in September 1779: "The various calamities which during the present year have befallen our crops of wheat, have reduced them so very low as to leave us little more than seed for the ensuing year, were it to be solely applied to that purpose."

Edmund Randolph wrote to James Madison, lamenting the very wet winter of 1782–83: "As a farmer, I have much to complain of violent and excessive rains, which have fallen throughout this winter. The necessary preparations for the early crops have not, I believe, been made any where, and a scanty harvest this year will amount to almost a famine next in our neighbourhood. At this time one snow would create greater havock among the cattle of Henrico than the enemy, so scarce is provender."

The Common Hall also regulated the sale of nonfood items within the city. All wood was to be sold by the cord; all hay, corn blades, or other fodder, by the pound. A member of the hustings court checked weights and measures, and a violator of these standards could have his goods given to the poor and pay a fine of twice their value.

Auctions, a popular means of selling many items in the city, usually took place on Henrico County court day, when a large number of people were in town. Galt's Tavern was a favorite place. Offerings included land, horses, slaves, a coal mine, a brewery, an assortment of broadcloths, flour, rum, and black pepper. Stephen Tankard, an ordinary-keeper, became public auctioneer as one of Common Hall's first official appointments in 1782.

Flour milling was one of the earliest industries in America and one of the most essential to independent survival. A number of mills existed in the Richmond area at the time of the Revolution. Samuel Overton operated a flour mill on lot no. 741, which he had purchased in the Byrd Lottery in 1772 for £700. The lot, a long triangular tract, extended seven-eighths of a mile along the north bank of the James River from what is to-day Fourteenth Street. Overton probably established his mill either over the rocks at the foot of Twelfth Street or perhaps farther up river, where Second and Third streets would reach the river if extended.

In 1777 Overton agreed to provide five hundred barrels of flour to Richard Adams, who was purchasing flour for the state. The fate of Overton's mill cannot be determined. It may have been destroyed in Arnold's raid in 1781, or the mill operated later by David Ross at the foot of Twelfth Street may have been the same as Overton's mill. In January 1784 a flood washed away Ross's mill, which stood over the river, and with it the miller, his assistant, three thousand bushels of wheat, and a quantity of flour.

Any center of trade, with the consequent traffic in ships, re-quired certain auxiliary industries. Ropemaking became more important in Richmond after the British burned the ropeworks at Norfolk in 1776. The pressing necessities of war, as well as trade, required rope, and during the Revolution the Richmond area supported three ropewalks—two in the city and one at nearby Warwick. Hemp for the rope came from the western part of the state. The ropeworks also produced sailcloth.

In August 1777 Archibald Cary and Company announced the opening of a new "Ropery" at Richmond. The company ad-vertised in the *Virginia Gazette* for a manager, who would be allowed to purchase part interest in the ropewalk, and "two or three good spinners." All would be furnished dwelling houses.

Located on Shockoe Hill, this ropeworks became known as

the Chatham Rope Yard Company. In addition to Cary, Turner Southall and James Buchanan had some financial interest in the operation, as did William Dandridge, Jr., the superintendent. In June 1779 Dandridge advertised in the *Virginia Gazette* that shipmasters could buy all types of rigging at the Chatham Rope Yard. Inflation had become so bad, however, that goods would no longer be sold on credit and prices on orders of rigging would not be set until the time of delivery.

A second privately owned rope company, known as the Richmond Ropewalk, stood in the east end of Richmond. It probably occupied land in what is today Fulton, bounded by Williamsburg Avenue, and Main, Nicholson, and Louisiana streets. James Marsden was manager in 1778, and Samuel Coleman in 1783. Set afire by an arsonist, Richmond Ropewalk partially burned in November 1783, but temporary repairs allowed business to continue as usual.

Benedict Arnold reported having burned a ropewalk in Richmond in January 1781. Because of its location on Shockoe Hill near other buildings that the British burned, the Chatham Rope Yard seems most likely to have been the victim. Other evidence supporting this view is the fact that Lafayette quartered his troops in the ropewalks in the east end of Richmond a few months later.

In an effort to meet the increased wartime demand for leather goods, two tanneries came into existence in the Richmond area. One, a privately owned tannery capable of receiving 1,500 hides, occupied land leased from the trustees of Richmond in 1777. The second, at Warwick, was related to the public ropewalks there.

The largest manufacturing operation in the Richmond area during the Revolution was the Westham foundry, established and owned by the State of Virginia. It stood on the north bank of the James River about one mile below the village of Westham and slightly downriver from Williams Island.

The General Assembly had decided on a site at the head of the falls of the James River and had purchased the three and one-half acre foundry site from John Ballendine. Ballendine intended to build a canal around the falls of the James to the Shockoe warehouses in Richmond. The foundry would have the right to free navigation on the canal and expected to use water from the canal to turn a boring mill.

By November 1778, after a little more than two years of planning and construction, the foundry was complete, including not only four double stacks, eight air furnaces, and a boring mill, but probably also the manager's dwelling and cabins for the workers. By March 1779 the owners had recruited enough workers, both slave and free, to begin the regular work of the foundry.

However, Ballendine never completed the canal, and the lack of water hindered operation of the boring mill. Nevertheless, the foundry produced both military and civilian goods. Military supplies included cannon, both four-pounders and six-pounders, cannonballs, grapeshot, grape cannisters, and swivels. Civilian items included handirons, flatirons, anvils, wagon boxes, spades and shovels, sledgehammmers, and spikes and nails. Bars and plates used in building the Westham air furnaces were cast on the spot. For the Hunter Iron Works at Fredericksburg, Westham foundry made three hammers, each weighing five hundred pounds.

Despite the fact that the foundry never reached its potential in output, it was producing enough military supplies to disturb the British. When Arnold invaded Richmond January 5, 1781, his main target for destruction was the Westham foundry.

A number of other small industries operated in the Richmond area during the Revolution. In 1777 John Mayo located a brewery and distillery at Manchester. The operation consisted of two stills and three coppers, one of which had a capacity of three hundred gallons. He advertised in the *Virginia Gazette* for a qualified, experienced superintendent, with an offer of partnership for the right man. Another brewery, located at Westham, was partly owned by a widow whose intercession saved it from destruction by Arnold's troops. The state prohibited the making of "spirituous liquors" from February to October 1779 because the distilleries consumed such a large quantity of grains, which were in short supply.

The partnership of Archibald Cary and Jacob Rubsamen manufactured gunpowder at a powder mill that Schoepf described as "the first in America." Rubsamen, a Jewish Bavarian chemist, had come to Manchester from New Jersey. On

May 7, 1777, the Council of State of Virginia agreed to buy from Cary and Rubsamen any quantity of gunpowder fit for muskets up to ten thousand pounds. Rubsamen also manufactured a large amount of saltpeter used in making gunpowder. He taught people in the back settlements of Virginia to make saltpeter.

In 1781, Arnold blew up the powder mill, just after Cary had sold Rubsamen full ownership. It probably occupied the old Murchies Mill site on Pocoshock Creek in Chesterfield County. Besides the mill, Rubsamen lost a large amount of gunpowder, a larger quantity of saltpeter, four thousand pounds of brimstone, and all his utensils.

Although—according to Jefferson's slave Isaac—only two brick houses stood within the city in 1780, virtually every structure used brick in the foundation or cellar walls. Bricks could be manufactured almost anywhere, depending on the availability of suitable materials. In 1783 the Common Hall granted the unusual request of James Geddy, John Smith, and Benjamin Lewis: they could make bricks in the streets if they agreed to level the street in the process. Bricks were also manufactured at the Chatham Rope Yard on Shockoe Hill, and bricks for the foundry were made at the site. Two residents listed their occupation as bricklayer or mason, Obadiah Clarke and Henry Anderson.

Fish was an important part of the diet, especially for Richmond's poorer people. While many caught their own fish, commercial fisheries, described as "very lucrative," operated on either side of the river at the falls. Herring and shad teemed there in the spring.

The number and variety of craftsmen in the Richmond area increased during the revolutionary period. While carpenters and woodworkers made up the largest segment of this group, the number of blacksmiths, leatherworkers, and silversmiths also increased. Nineteen persons, 13 percent of those listing a trade, indicated a form of carpentry as their occupation in the tax list of 1782. In addition, two black carpenter slaves who were hired out also appear in the tax list, and two journeymen and three apprentices were learning carpentry.

Of the nineteen men involved in woodworking occupations, four residents listed their trade as "carpenter": Milton Ford,

Tanus Tate, John Hawkins, and Samuel Stewart. Five listed their occupation as "joiner," a more specialized carpenter who did interior finishing work on mouldings, stairways, and windows, and made simple furniture. Alexander Montgomery, Edward Newman, James Hutchins, John Richardson, and Robert Sheerman were joiners when the tax list was compiled in October 1782. Four men, John Bryan, John Murphy, Peter Maxxie, and Samuel Scherer, listed their occupation as "chairmaker." John Clark was the city's one "cabinet maker." Only three men, William Franklin, William Kerson, and John Liggon, pursued the important trade of cooper, making the various wooden containers—barrels, kegs, tubs—used for storing and shipping merchandise as well as for farm and household use.

Another industry of importance in the Richmond area was shipbuilding. The 1782 tax list names Isaac Armistead and William Borum as ship carpenters. In November 1783 Arthur Smith advertised a large double schooner, fifty-nine feet long, which would be ready for sale in December. He also had on the docks near Richmond, more than half finished, a "large double decked vessel built of the very best white oak," which would be ready in June.

The demand for skilled weavers, shoemakers, and tailors or seamstresses increased with the boycotting of English goods in 1775, as shown by the number of newspaper advertisements for these skills.

The extent of success in filling these positions cannot be determined. None of the city's inhabitants listed weaving as an occupation in 1782, though many households certainly must have included weavers. Three women listed their occupation as "seamstress," three women as "mantua maker," six men as "tailor," and six men as "shoemaker" in 1782. Robert Gilbert, a maker of boots and shoes in Williamsburg, announced in 1783 that he was moving to Richmond to carry on his business.

Four Richmonders listed their occupation as "tanner" in 1782, and a number of saddlers in the city made finished products from the leather. Other skilled craftsmen plying their art in Richmond included three silversmiths, two watchmakers, three blacksmiths, two potters, and a wagon maker.

The entire economic life of Richmond during the Revolution

suffered from constant inflation of prices and a steady decrease in value of the paper money in circulation. In January of 1777 the ratio of the value of paper money to that of gold and silver stood at one and a half to one. It widened to four to one by the end of the year, increased to six to one in 1778, and jumped in 1779 to forty to one.

In 1780 the price of tobacco at Richmond warehouses increased from £30 per hogshead to £75 per hogshead, and the ratio of paper money to coin rose to seventy-five to one. But in 1781 the ratio zoomed to one thousand to one. People began demanding their pay in tobacco rather than in the rapidly depreciating currency, and thus tobacco became the major medium of exchange. By January 1783 money had almost disappeared from circulation in Richmond.

From September 1781 through 1783, however, Richmond trade improved. In September 1781 a ship arrived with much-needed salt. A petition from a group of merchants and trading companies observed that "the commerce of this country is beginning to revive." Alexander Nelson advertised in January and again in June of 1782 that he had for sale at the "Brick Store" near the tobacco warehouses a large assortment of European and West Indian goods that he had just imported.

By June 1783 the British were again involved in trade with Richmond; several ships had arrived from Bristol. As a result, the price of goods had moved down and the price of tobacco had gone up to forty shillings a hundredweight, almost double the price offered in February 1783. Nelson, Heron, and Company advertised in September 1783 that they had just imported "a large and general assortment of merchandize suitable to the season." William Pennock announced in October that he had imported a "a large general assortment of European and East Indian goods." Commerce was moving in both directions.

Reflecting the changing trade conditions as the war drew to a close, three Richmond trading companies dissolved their partnerships in 1782 and 1783. The "co-partnership" of Hunter, Banks, and Company, formed in August 1780, provided primarily military supplies during the war, especially for Generals Greene and Lafayette and for David Ross, purchasing agent for Virginia. The partnership dissolved in August 1782. In October 1783 William Pennock announced the dissolution of the partnership of William Pennock and Company. The demise of Benjamin Harrison, Jr., and Company was also announced in October.

The war had given these Virginia merchants the opportunity to participate in foreign trade, so effectively dominated by the British before the war. But because of the absence of British trade, goods had been scarce and whatever could be imported met with an eager market. As the war ended, privateering was no longer legal and British ships returned to trade. Virginia merchants found themselves again at a disadvantage.

CHAPTER NINE

The Loyalties of Richmonders

"A TORY has been properly defined to be a traitor in thought, but not in deed," wrote Thomas Jefferson. Americans applied the term both to persons who affirmed loyalty to the king and to those who simply refused to swear allegiance to the United States. Any who engaged in overt activity against the United States in effect crossed the line from toryism or loyalism to treason. British merchants and factors in Virginia, whose loyalty and nationality properly lay with Great Britain, perhaps should be viewed as alien enemies. Technically, the Virginia government considered all defectors as "enemies to America."

The records show very few professed loyalists, tories, or nonjurors in the Richmond area. The *Virginia Gazette* in January 1776 published a list of ten loyalists in Richmond and nine in Manchester who had already left the colony or were about to leave.

Thomas Reid, a Scottish merchant in Richmond, along with Archibald McKendrick and James Watts, departed before the Virginia Assembly passed antiloyalist laws. Reid left an agent, however, who was able to collect part of his debts. One of the most prominent loyalists, Archibald Govan, had to leave the state by order of the county court, an action upheld by the Council of State. For their own protection, some merchants published their intent to leave in the newspapers while winding up their affairs.

Some Virginians especially suspected the loyalty of two groups, other than British merchants and factors: Quakers and Negroes. Holding that "a Treasonable Correspondence has been carried on for some Time by the Society of Quakers" in Pennsylvania, the Council of State felt that "there is great Reason to suspect that the same may have in some Degree extended to the Members of that Society" in Virginia. Accordingly it resolved:

that the Governor be advised to write to the first or any other Magistrate of the Counties of Henrico, Nansemond, Hanover, Loudoun, & any other County where meetings of the Quakers are held to inform them of the Grounds of Suspicion, & requesting them to use their best Endeavours to gain Information in whose Custody the Records of the meetings of the Society remains, to issue their Warrants for the Seizing the same & if any such Treasonable practices or misprision thereof shall be thereby discovered that they issue their Warrants for apprehending the persons who may appear to be concerned therein, & have them proceeded against according to Law.

Except for a group from Pennsylvania interned at Winchester "as Enemies to the Independence of America," Virginia did not deal further with the Quakers. Few Quakers had ever made their home in Virginia, and most of those, at the time of the Revolution, had settled in central Virginia, considered relatively safe from enemy invasion. Furthermore, it seems that, contrary to the Council's belief, the Virginia Quakers supported the American cause.

Many blacks at the start of the war had gone off to join the British in the eastern part of the state. Whites feared that others would "follow their Example & be Instruments in the Hands of our Enemies committing Robberies & other Depredations on their former Masters, and other Inhabitants of that part of this State." The Assembly empowered the governor to remove both blacks and whites as he saw fit to the "interior" part of the state.

A number of slaves employed by the state defected to the enemy during the British invasion. When Arnold came to Richmond, four slaves in James Anderson's repair shop left with the British army. Fifteen slaves employed at the public ropewalk at Warwick went off with Cornwallis's army in June 1781. One of the public slaves, who had worked at the Westham Foundry, returned and gave himself up to Turner Southall, who then sought reemployment for him in the repair shop.

The records are scant as to defection of any white servants. Most of the few in Virginia at the time of the Revolution (excluding tutors and apprentices), probably worked in the service of British merchants. The *Virginia Gazette* advertised for a servant who had absconded from Richmond on December 3, 1775: "Run away . . . an *English* servant man, named RALPH CHILLINGSWORTH, of the middle stature;" he was "slim made" and had had the smallpox, "is very fond of spiritous liquors, a plaisterer by trade, and very sensible fellow." It was feared that he would attempt to board a British warship at Norfolk. A forty shillings reward was offered to whomever should apprehend him.

Central Virginia had few persons who flaunted their loyalism. The vigilante-style committees of safety seem to have effectively intimidated anyone who might have had such notions. Perhaps some Virginians learned the value of silence as early as 1774, when threats were made against any violators of the nonimportation-of-tea agreement. At that time Archibald Cary of Ampthill, while serving in the legislature at Williamsburg, erected a pole opposite Raleigh Tavern upon which was hung "a bag of feathers and under it a bucket of tar."

Only one instance of physical intimidation of a loyalist in Richmond is recorded. Unfortunately, the victim, a shoemaker of uncommon spunk, remains unnamed. In May 1777, General Francis Nash and a force of North Carolina Continentals marched through Richmond on their way to join Washington's army. Suddenly from the door of a shoe shop they heard, "Hurrah for King George!" No one paid much attention. But when the North Carolinians halted in the woods just outside the town the little shoemaker came up, and again began to hurrah for the king.

When the General and his aids mounted and started, he still followed them, hurrahing for King George. Upon which the General ordered him to be taken back to the river and ducked. We brought along rope, which we tied about the middle, round his middle, and seesawed him backwards and forwards until we had him nearly drowned, but every time he got his head above water he would cry for King George. The General having then ordered him to be tarred and feathered, a feather bed was taken from his own house, where were his wife and four likely daughters crying and beseeching their father to hold his tongue, but still he would not. We tore the bed open and knocked the top out of a tar barrel, into which we plunged him headlong. He was then drawn out by the heels and rolled in the feathers until he was a sight but still he would hurrah for King George. The General now ordered him to be drummed out of the West end of town, and told him expressly that if he plagued him any more in that way he would have him shot. So we saw no more of the shoemaker.

In 1779 Virginia began in earnest to confiscate and sell property belonging to loyalist refugees and British subjects. That same year the legislature banished all loyalist refugees and forbade their reentrance. In 1782 the Virginia Assembly declared that all British subjects returning to the state were to be regarded as prisoners of war. In accordance with a policy recommended by Congress, it also directed that confiscated estates be sold for the benefit of troops of the Virginia line.

By 1780 the authorities increasingly sent persons accused of disloyalty, whether convicted or not, to Richmond. The British invasion of 1781 flushed many loyalists into the open, especially in the lower counties along the coast and on the Eastern Shore. It was considered a possibility that many persons in this area would have actively engaged themselves in the British cause, but the British army moved "without any confidence" and treated the loyalists with contempt in the period leading up to Yorktown.

In the fall of 1781, Richmond received a number of loyalists for incarceration. Among these, the most important was the Reverend John Lyon, rector of St. George's Parish in Accomac County. Lyon had been sentenced to five years imprisonment by a local court-martial for aiding the enemy. His disaffection to the American cause extended even to the point of exhorting militia not to take arms against the British. After brief confinement in Richmond, Lyon was released, giving security and promising that he would not go any closer than forty miles to a British post.

Following Yorktown, the jail at Richmond became so crowded that some prisoners had to be released on bail. Many of the new prisoners were loyalists taken at Yorktown. They and other notorious loyalists were sent to Richmond for trial, largely because, as Governor Harrison noted, it was "impossible to procure proper Gentlemen to act as Judges" of the local courts of oyer and terminer.

In December 1781 the purge of loyalists began in earnest in Richmond. Even two tavern keepers in the town who had participated in the rebel cause, Richard Hogg and Gabriel Galt, and two Richmond merchants, John Cox and Zachariah Rowland, suffered arrest. Each had to post bond of £1,000 in specie to appear for trial before the "Supreme Executive" on the charge of disloyalty. They may have appeared before the Council or the General Court to explain their alleged disaffection, but they did not stand trial.

Some of the manacled prisoners brought in from the lower counties and from Yorktown faced the full weight of prosecution for high treason. Kept in irons, they nearly starved. Richard Burnley, captured at Yorktown, was eventually released, but died five days later from the maltreatment he had received in the Richmond jail.

On December 4, 1781, the Council issued a special commission of oyer and terminer, constituting Paul Carrington, Peter Lyon, and William Fleming as judges. They were to meet at the Henrico Court House on Tuesday, December 11, 1781, to try thirty-six persons imprisoned in the Richmond jail, "there being just cause to suspect that all the forementioned persons are disaffected to the Independance of the American States and attached to their Enemies." Presumably the special court discharged most of the accused on their promise or surety of good behavior. No convictions for treason resulted.

The Henrico court records indicate that action was taken against a few of the accused. John Logan and Edward Murphy, charged with voluntarily joining and adhering to the enemy, received a jury trial and were found innocent. John Royall, tried on the same charge and convicted, received a twelve-month jail sentence. Basil Jackson, a Maryland Loyalist taken at Yorktown, came to trial on a writ of *habeas corpus.* No witnesses appearing against him, he was released. Thomas Barnette (Barret?) tried for treason in April 1782, was acquitted.

In the spring of 1782 the General Court conducted the trials of persons accused of disloyalty and treason. It tried the Reverend William Andrews of Southampton County for treason, for which the law provided the death penalty. The court did not convict him, and the Council allowed him to leave the state providing he did not return.

Meeting at the Henrico Court House in Richmond on April 5, 1782, the General Court did convict of treason Robert Smith, a laborer from Hampshire County, who had led an antitax riot, and James Hughes, a butcher from the city of Richmond. The court sentenced them to be hanged.

Many Richmonders sympathized with the plight of their neighborhood butcher. On his behalf, twenty-eight of them—including Gabriel Galt, Robert Mitchell, Robert Boyd, Serafino Formicola, and James Buchanan—petitioned the House of

Delegates for clemency on the basis of extenuating circumstances. Hughes and Smith were both eventually pardoned. Their execution dates had been set far enough distant that the legislature had time to review the verdict.

Another oyer and terminer session of the General Court, meeting in Richmond during May and June 1782, condemned six persons to death, three for high treason: James Lamb, Joshua Hopkins and John (also referred to as James) Caton, all of Princess Anne County. The three traitors petitioned the General Assembly for a pardon, thereby setting in motion Virginia's first constitutional crisis. Two questions were raised. Who, if anyone, should decide on the constitutionality of an act of the Assembly (the treason law of 1776)? And who should resolve a conflict between the House of Delegates and the Senate? In this case, one house voted for the pardon, and the other did not.

The General Court entered the fray but could not decide either on the constitutionality of the treason law or on its own power of judicial review. So the case, which became known as *Caton* v. *Commonwealth*, went to the Court of Appeals. Excitement ran high in Richmond. From the members of the Assembly, arriving for a new session, to the man in the street, the case was the foremost topic of conversation. Many persons wondered if the Court of Appeals could properly review a criminal case, let alone the constitutionality of a law.

Attorney General Edmund Randolph, only twenty-nine years old and himself the son of a tory, presented the case for the commonwealth. Andrew Ronald, a twenty-eight-year-old Scotsman who had settled in Richmond, served as chief counsel for the prisoners. Samuel Hardy, a popular young lawyer and member of the Assembly, assisted in the defense. William Nelson, John Francis Mercer, and St. George Tucker (the oldest lawyer in court at age thirty) participated as *amici curiae*.

Although disagreeing on various points of law, six judges to two upheld the constitutionality of the Treason Act, which seemed to seal the fate of the condemned men. The prisoners, however, submitted another petition to the Assembly, which this time proved successful in both the Senate and the House of Delegates.

Lamb and Hopkins received pardons on condition only that

they leave the state in two months. Caton and three other men sentenced to death for treason in the October session of the general court were pardoned on condition that they serve in the Continental army. These four had to report for induction into the army in Richmond, where Capt. Samuel Hogg ordered them to report for duty at Winchester. Instead, three of the pardoned traitors deserted and were never heard from again.

Other persons convicted of treason in the October General Court were also eventually released. John Holland and Demsey Butler of Nansemond had close calls, however. On November 29 both men were taken to the gallows, just outside the city, along with a condemned murderer and four horse thieves. There the horse thieves received pardons on condition of joining the army. The murderer was hanged. Holland and Butler already stood "under the gallows." But before they could stretch hemp a reprieve arrived, postponing execution until the next session of the Assembly could review their case.

The treason trials and punishment of tories seemed to stimulate an accusatory mood in Richmond, whereby neighbor denounced neighbor for being soft on toryism. Like other witch-hunts before and since, officials found out only too well how easily the fires of hatred, searching for scapegoats, could be fanned. Undoubtedly for this reason the government slowed prosecutions for treason. After all, Virginians had fought first of all against tyranny, and in a sober mood would not want to substitute another kind for it.

Two letters late in 1782 to the publisher of the Richmond newspaper reveal how far out of hand the witch-hunt was getting. The initial writer to the paper had accused another of being a tory for his position on paper money. The second correspondent retorted: "I find it a maxim in these times with designing men, when they propose measures for public view, if their true motives should be exposed, and their dark designs discovered, immediately to cry out *a Tory! a Tory!* thinking by that means to envelope truth in the garb of Toryism."

As the government cooled its tory hunt, only John Holland remained in the Richmond jail under sentence of death for treason. In December 1782, the General Court failed to convict two persons accused of treason. Similarly in January 1783, it acquitted Isaac Riddle in what was probably the last treason trial of the Revolution in Virginia. The legislature finally pardoned Holland in May 1783.

That ended the brief wave of prosecutions for treason well before it reached anything like a reign of terror. Indeed, Virginians could be proud that the state did not put to death any-one charged with treason.

But recrimination of a different kind against tories exacted a heavy toll. A substantial amount of loyalist property was confiscated and sold in Virginia, although the precise amount cannot be determined. The state auditor's accounts from 1779 to 1795 show a total value of £3,041,167 in sales of confiscated property. Except for £13,126 of that amount, the state received payment before 1782 in depreciated currency. Hence the state realized a minimal return from the sale of the property.

Not all the sequestered property went on sale, however. Various branches and departments of the state government in-stalled themselves in certain Richmond warehouses and homes confiscated from British firms and sympathizers.

William Cuninghame and Company, Glasgow merchants, suffered the most extensive confiscation. The firm, dating back to the 1720s, had acquired operations in fourteen different places in Virginia by the time of the Revolution.

Another Glasgow firm, Henderson, McCaul, and Company, also had an extensive trade and much property in Virginia. Among other properties the company owned "a Set of Warehouses adjoining the Town of Richmond . . . known by the Name of Byrd's or Shockoe's Warehouses, from which Property by the Lodgments of Tobacco they drew a considera-ble Annual Revenue." Cornwallis burned the Shockoe warehouses, resulting in the total loss of the tobacco.

Certain individuals had their property in Richmond and Henrico County confiscated, among them James McDowell, French Crawford, and Ninian Minzies. Robert Baine's six-hundred-acre plantation in Henrico County and a "Tenement" in Richmond were confiscated, along with slaves, furniture, and "Stock of all kinds." The state purchased part of the escheated property, and various citizens bought the rest.

Baine had left Virginia in 1775, after fifteen years residence, and the confiscation took place in his absence. Returning from

Great Britain in 1780, Baine petitioned the legislature for restoration of citizenship and property. He claimed to be "a peaceable Man" and "long determined to spend his life in Virginia." And neither any law enacted during his residence nor "the Spirit of any Act of Assembly passed since" made him ineligible for restitution. The Assembly found that Baine's claim was reasonable and recommended to the governor that his property be returned to him and that he be compensated for rent, hire of his slaves, and damages done to his land. Among other property, Baine recovered houses in Richmond and received compensation for their rent.

In summer 1783 the final peace treaty, soon forthcoming, held out the prospect of loyalists being allowed to return and to recover confiscated property. Not all Richmonders and Henricoans were pleased. Motivated, so it seems, by greed as well as patriotism, fifty-three citizens signed a petition in opposition to "the most distant probability of admitting to an equal participation of those Blessings" persons "who have hazarded nothing." Those who had not given "assurance of Attachment to our Interests" and those who had left Virginia should not recover their property. Two hundred eighty-nine freeholders of Hanover County submitted a similar petition.

The sixth article in the Treaty of Paris between Great Britain and the United States forbade any "future confiscations." The Virginia Assembly accepted this provision on the condition that the treaty did not extend to any suit pending in court initiated before the ratification of the treaty.

Some loyalists began to return by midsummer 1782, contrary to the law. Edmund Randolph in July rendered an opinion that British subjects who returned to Virginia without authorization might be treated as "enemies." But still, he said, they were citizens, "supposed to be innocent until conviction and are at liberty to risque themselves upon a trial for life or death." With Virginia soon to give up the idea of punishment of tories, the presumption of innocence until proven guilty paved the way for tories to return practically with impunity.

One beneficiary of this new latitude, a Captain Waterman, had commanded a ship in the London trade before the war. In London at the outbreak of the war because of the death of an uncle, Waterman eventually made his way back to Virginia. Appearing before the Council of State at Richmond in December 1782, he asked to become a citizen, and presumably received permission to stay.

As late as July 1783, however, Governor Harrison issued a proclamation ordering departure, according to the law, for any loyalists who had returned. But in October 1783 the Assembly, with the urging of Patrick Henry, allowed the admission to Virginia of British subjects who had not borne arms with Great Britain. The Assembly also passed during the October 1783 session a law suspending executions on judgments against loyalist property for four months until the next meeting of the Assembly.

Not until 1787 did the Assembly repeal the prohibition on the recovery of British debts, and then with the stipulation that the law would not be operative until the British complied with their part of the treaty. The Virginia legislature insisted that no private debts be paid in England until the British government reimbursed Virginians for the freed slaves.

Virginia had been fortunate in not experiencing a long period of invasion by the enemy and also in enjoying relative political unity at the start of the war. Thus the commonwealth escaped much of the internal enmity that characterized other states. Virginia had its witch-hunt, to be sure. Some loyalists, confined for brief periods toward the end of the war, lost their civil rights and suffered the inhumane conditions of the Richmond prison. Many émigrés elected to return, however, and did so unmolested. Only a few paid the price of becoming permanent exiles. Overall, Virginia had a moderate record in the treatment of loyalists.

CHAPTER TEN

Those Who Fought

THE PATRIOTISM of Richmonders in the Revolution differed little, if any, from that of other Virginians. Some used it as an excuse to level wild accusations against their neighbors. All too few allowed it to propel them into serving their country through thick and thin. Desertion or, more often, simple failure to show up when summoned, plagued state and Continental services alike.

Gen. John Peter Muhlenberg, one of Washington's most valued officers, took command of recruiting Continental troops in Virginia in February 1780. Making Richmond his recruiting headquarters, Muhlenberg used an officer "who rides Circuit" to gather recruits "once in two months." In April, after such a collection, only fifty recruits were obtained and were immediately sent southward.

The general lamented that most of the "draughted soldiers in different parts of the country" were so "dispersed" and had enlisted for so short a period of time it was not worth the time and expense to muster them into the Continental service. He accepted only those who enlisted for the duration of the war.

In fact, Muhlenberg objected to Richmond as the central depot for receiving Continental troops. Governor Jefferson recommended Chesterfield Court House, and Muhlenberg agreed. Thus Chesterfield Court House and sometimes nearby Petersburg, became the main receiving center.

The Congressional Board of War, however, still regarded Richmond as the receiving depot. Baron de Kalb arrived in Richmond on May 22 to take charge of troops to be sent to General Gates. He found troops being collected neither at Richmond nor at Chesterfield Court House, but at Petersburg instead.

By mid-July, only 1,438 Virginia troops had joined Gates's command. Of 624 Henrico County militia on the rosters, 83 were drafted for service in the South, and of that number, 14 did not appear. Thus, 69 Henricoans served in the southern army at that time.

Under an act of October 1780 providing for new levies for the Continental army, Henrico County raised thirty-eight men (thirteen for the duration of the war, three for three years, and twenty-two drafted). Two of the inductees "abscounded," and two remained in the county company; therefore thirty-four of the thirty-eight were actually "delivered."

The British landing under General Leslie at Portsmouth in October 1780 caused a temporary halt in the sending of troops to the Southern Army. The militia force organized under Thomas Nelson and sent to check Leslie could do little; the artillery and ammunition it needed had been carried to Richmond.

Further to meet the emergency of the British invasion, the government called up ten thousand militia—one-third (later changed to one-fourth) of the number to come from twenty-one counties, including Henrico. The militia turnout was gratifying. Gen. George Weedon, who had come down from Fredericksburg to assist in assembling the militia at Richmond, reported that the counties were supplying their quotas and "not one County has been oblig'd to Draught. . . ."

The regular troops, however, were scattered and disorganized. General Steuben reported that he found troops in and around Richmond "under a Variety of Commanders." Viewing a military parade in Richmond on December 1, he counted only 340 men of Lawson's corps of short-term volunteers, far below its full strength of nearly 800 men. Following Leslie's departure and in accord with a resolution of the House of Delegates, Steuben discharged the whole corps. He also had discharged 200 riflemen, who were three-month men, and had "pressed the Discharge of the Militia and other Corps who were then only exhausting our already too scanty Magazines."

When the British force under Arnold moved up the James in January the Council of State took emergency action, calling out the militia from twenty-three counties. One-half of the militiamen of Henrico, Hanover, and Goochland counties and one-fourth from Fluvanna, Albemarle, and Amherst counties were to rendezvous at Richmond. On January 4, a second call went out for *all* men able to bear arms from Henrico, Hanover,

Goochland, Powhatan, and Chesterfield to rendezvous at Westham. Militiamen were to go to a rendezvous even if not organized into companies.

Only 150 Continentals at Chesterfield Court House were fit for duty at the time of the invasion. They were ordered to Petersburg, then to Westham, and finally on January 5 to Manchester to join about 200 militia there. Thus, few troops of any sort could oppose Arnold's march into Richmond. Militia numbers grew, however, as Arnold began his retreat. Then, after the British troops left Richmond, the Henrico militia went home; not one stayed to join the regulars.

General Greene was not surprised that so few troops opposed Arnold. He had observed a month before, on his way through Virginia to assume the southern command, that Virginians were taking "very trifling" measures. "All the way through the country, as I passed, I found the people engaged in matters of interest and in pursuit of pleasure, almost regardless of their danger. Public credit totally lost, and every man excusing himself from giving the least aid to Government, from an apprehension that they would get no return for any advances."

As Phillips advanced up the James in April 1781: crisis again. The county lieutenants of Henrico and six other counties received orders to "assemble every man of your County able to bear arms," for a two-month tour of duty. Militia stayed in the field during Cornwallis's invasion. Throughout the summer, Henrico and other counties kept one-fourth of their militia in the field "by regular Rotation." In Henrico this was done without difficulty.

The story was different for army volunteers. According to a roll of county contributions of six-month men for the period preceding November 1, 1781 Henrico County "delivered" 3 men of the 216 reporting from the various counties; from all the counties, there was a shortage of 370 men.

State guard forces were still another matter. At the beginning of the war, the Virginia government recognized the need to have military units solely for guarding key places in the state. In May 1778 the General Assembly created the State Garrison Regiment of eight companies. Originally its main purpose was to guard harbors and ports. In 1780 a detachment of the Gar-

rison Regiment provided a guard for the General Assembly in
Richmond. During Arnold's invasion, Lt. Churchill Gibbs commanded the guard in Richmond and was captured by the
enemy.

After the invasion, a few troops were kept in Richmond as a
garrison. On March 28, 1781, the governor and the Council appointed Captain Hamilton as "Town major" in Richmond—
Hamilton "being an old officer and belonging to the new regiment." Among his duties were to "take care of the various calls
of the garrison, transient troops &c.," and also to serve as
superintendent of public works. It was expected that he would
take some of the load off Commisioner Davies's shoulders.

After Yorktown, to protect military stores that Washington
ordered deposited in Richmond, the Virginia government
pressed into service a "Militia Guard" of twenty-five men from
Henrico County "until a sufficient number of the State Regiment can be had." For the several months that the stores
remained in Richmond, the Henrico militia performed this
duty.

Soldiers from the First State Regiment did arrive in Richmond, but they were used to guard the jail and the courthouse.
At one time three of the twenty-eight soldiers assigned to guard
the jail and the courthouse were in jail themselves for abetting
the escape of two prisoners.

In September 1782 the Common Hall of Richmond asked
the Commissioner of War to remove "the present Guard over
the Jail, it having been guilty of great irregularities," and to
bring a detachment of troops from Yorktown to Richmond.

Military actions involve not just units of various types but individuals, who may be officers or ordinary soldiers and who
have—or had—names. Unfortunately, not much is known of
those individuals—Richmonders or others—who did serve and
sacrifice in the defense of Virginia's capital city.

Personnel records of volunteer and militia units—the former
going through repeated reorganizations as short-termers
constantly arrived and left for home, the latter repeatedly
mustered and then disbanded—are neither clear nor complete.
During the invasion crisis almost every able-bodied white male
adult must have seen at least a few days of service; but at that
moment no one seems to have bothered about record keeping.
And in any case, Arnold destroyed all the earlier local archives.

Although carefully culled from all known sources, therefore, the following listings must be viewed as only partial and uncertain. The first list contains the names of the more prominent Continental and state staff and other military-related officials who did not reside in Richmond but did serve in the area for part or all of the period 1780–82.

Anderson, James. Superintendent of the armorer and repair laboratory at Richmond and then at Westham.

Aylett, William. Commissary of Supplies; Deputy Commissary General of Purchases for the Southern Department and the state; Deputy Commissary General of Supplies for the state.

Bohannon, Ambrose. Commissary General of Military Stores for the state; Regimental Paymaster.

Brown, [Windsor?]. Commissary General of Provisions for the state; Assistant Commissary of Military Stores.

Brown, Thomas. Commissioner of the Navy.

Browne, John. Commissioner of the Provision Law.

Carrington, Lt. Col. Edward. Deputy Quartermaster General (hereafter DQMG) for the Southern Army.

Claiborne, Richard. DQMG for the Southern Army; Quartermaster (hereafter QM) for Virginia.

Davies, William. Commissioner of the War Office.

Day, Benjamin. State Agent.

Febiger, Col. Christian. Continental officer, forwarded supplies to the army.

Finnie, Col. William. DQMG for the Southern Department.

Fleming, William. Director of State Laboratory.

Forsythe, Maj. Robert. Commissary General of Purchases for the Southern Army; Continental Purchasing Commissary in Virginia.

Green, Capt. Berryman. Assistant Deputy QM (hereafter DQM) for the "Continent in the State of Virginia."

Harrison, Benjamin. Paymaster of Continental troops in Virginia.

Hay, William. Commercial Agent; briefly Acting Commissary of Public Stores, in absence of William Armistead.

Irish, Nathaniel. Continental Commissary of Military Stores in Virginia; one month as Acting Commissary of Military Stores for the state; in charge of Continental Laboratory (Westham).

Jones, Maj. Cadwalader. Appointed by Steuben "to receive the men and Stores" for the two legions at Petersburg and Chesterfield Court House—presumably occasionally in Richmond.

Jones, Joseph [?]. Deputy Field Commissary General of Military Stores (Manchester).

Kemp, James. QM, Virginia Garrison Regiment; Assistant Quartermaster General and Acting Quartermaster General (hereafter QMG).

Langbourne (Langborn), Lt. Col. William. DQMG (?).

Loyall, Paul. Commissioner of the Navy.

Mason, Mr. ———. Commissary.

Maxwell, James. Commissioner of the Navy.

Morris, Col. Richard. Appointed to settle accounts of the Commissioners of the Provision Law.

Munford, William Green. Deputy Commissary General of Issues in the state.

Muter, Col. George. Commissioner of the War Office.

Newman, Owen. Issuing Commissary at Richmond.

Newton, Thomas, Jr. Commissioner of the Navy.

Oliver, Capt. Lt. William. In charge of State Laboratory in Richmond.

Peyton, John. Clothier General for state troops; Superintendent of Military Stores, Arms, Ammunition.

Pierce, John. Commissary General of Provisions for state; Commissioner to settle accounts for district including Henrico.

Pryor, Capt. (Major) John. Commissary General of Military Stores for Southern Department; Commissary of Military Stores for the state.

Robertson, John. Superintendent, Commissary of Issues and Hides, and Acting Deputy Commissary of Issues.

Rose, William. DQMG at Fredericksburg, but occasionally in Richmond.

Ross, David. State Agent; State Commissary; afterwards a merchant in Richmond.

Russell, Capt. Charles. Assistant DQM (Continental).

Scott, Capt. ———. In charge of State Laboratory in Richmond.

Smith, Granville. Assistant QMG (state); State QM.

Smith, Thomas. Commercial Agent.

Southall, Stephen. DQMG; Brigade Major and QMG for the state.

Spiller, Capt. William. Commissary of Military Stores for the state.

Turner, Zephaniah. Commissioner to settle accounts of Virginia with the Continent.

Wood, Leighton. Solicitor of Virginia; ordered by General Assembly to prepare accounts of the state for a settlement with the Continent.

Young, Capt. Henry. QMG for the state.

The list that follows covers the entire war period and contains the names of prominent Henricoans who gave active—or at least more than desultory—service as officers. It indicates their rank and, where possible, their specific responsibility.

Adams, Richard. First Lieutenant, Henrico militia, October, 1781.

Ambler, Jacquelin. (State Treasurer). Served in Richmond militia.

Armistead, William. State Commissary of Stores, 1780–82.

Beckley, John. Mayor in 1783.

Bowles, David. Captain, Henrico militia, 1777.

Dabney, _____. Captain, Henrico Battalion, 1775–76.

DuVal, Daniel, Jr. Soldier in Captain DuVal's company (see below), recruiting in Henrico County, Jan. 1776.

DuVal, Samuel. Major, militia (earlier had served as sheriff and parish collector).

DuVal, William. Captain, Henrico District, 1775–76.

Ege, Samuel. Richmond militia; commissary.

Foushee, William. (Mayor of Richmond in 1782.) Surgeon, director of hospital at Richmond, Jan. 1782 to April 1783; also, as a magistrate, witnessed oaths of officers taking up commissions.

McKeand, John. Served in Richmond militia.

Mitchell, Robert. (Mayor of Richmond in 1784.) Second Lieutenant, Richmond militia, November 3, 1777.

Mosby, William. Ensign, Henrico militia, 1775; First Lieutentant, 5th Continental Line, February 24, 1776, and Captain, Dec. 18, 1776; resigned June 2, 1778; Major, militia, 1780; volunteer, cavalry, 1781.

Pleasants, John. Captain, recruiting officer in Henrico in March, 1776.

Prosser, Thomas. Captain, Henrico militia; 1775–76.
Selden, Miles, Jr. Captain, Henrico militia; chaplain, 1780.
Smith, James. From Henrico during early part of war; served as Second Lieutenant in the Virginia Continental Line.
Southall, Turner. Colonel, first served in 1776 in Elizabeth City District militia; commander of volunteer light dragoons "for the protection of the eastern frontiers" of Virginia, December 1780; 1781–83 in Henrico militia.
Woodson, Frederick. Resident, Henrico County; officer in State Garrison Regiment.
Younghusband, Isaac. Captain, Virginia navy; commanded *Mosquito* early 1776; resigned October 31, 1776.

Perhaps the leading revolutionary war hero buried in Richmond (Shockoe Hill Cemetery) is Major James Gibbons. Gibbons, who led a charge on Stony Point, New York, on July 15, 1779, served in the Pennsylvania Continental Line and came to Richmond after the war.

The Henrico County Court on October 13, 1781, nominated the following eight men "as fit persons to be commissioned Officers" of the militia. The governor and the Council of State were to make the final selection.

Turpin, John	Captain
Price, John	Captain
Adams, Richard	First Lieutenant
Hollman, Nathaniel	First Lieutenant
Turpin, Sugly	Second Lieutenant
Johnson, Benjamin	Second Lieutenant
Giles, William	Ensign
Hondle, Hezekiah	Ensign

Richard Sharpe served as captain of the militia in 1782. When he resigned, the court appointed John Royston in September 1782 to succeed him. At the same time it named Benjamin Goode as first lieutenant, Richard Sharpe, second lieutenant, and John Woodfin (or Woodson), ensign.

During the January 1781 invasion, twelve Henricoans signed up "to serve our Country as Cavalry" for a period not exceeding six months and on the condition that the government would supply "the necessary accoutrements" and pay: John Pleasants, Samuel Woodson, Isham Woodson, Samuel Pleasants, Matthew Pleasant, Pleasants Younghusband, Isaac Pleasants, John Cheadle, William Hay, Robert Green, Phillip Pleasant, and William Mosby. Governor Jefferson agreed to their terms.

The table that follows contains the names of persons taken into the Continental service as noncommissioned officers and privates who can be identified as residents of Richmond or of Henrico County. The names come from Continental military rolls (1780–81).

At Richmond in July 1783, Lt. David Mann, commander of the guards at Richmond, recruited the following into the First Virginia State Regiment: William Cooper, James Napper, William Granger, David Jones, John Jane, Simon Shaw, Thomas Gibbons, Jesse Loden, Michael Jordan, Sylvanus Seely, and John Steward. Michael Jordan is the only one in the above list who can be identified as being from Henrico County, but probably all the men recruited in Richmond were from the immediate area.

On April 1, 1783, the House of Delegates sent a resolution to the governor to stop recruiting for the Continental service. At that time less than two-hundred Virginians were serving in the Southern Army; several hundred were stationed elsewhere in the state and at Fort Pitt. Discharges proceeded rapidly. As in the years 1780–81, when militia who had been pressed into field service went to Richmond to obtain their discharges, so in 1782–83, returning Continentals often came to Richmond to receive "a portion of their pay" and their discharges.

With most of the fighting over, Richmond officialdom celebrated the Declaration of Independence on July 4, 1782. The governor entertained the officials of the state and of Richmond, prominent citizens, and officers of the army who were in town. The gathering drank the following thirteen patriotic toasts: to the U.S., to the king of France, to the queen and dauphin of France, to the king of Spain, to the United Netherlands, to General Washington, to Count Rochambeau, to General Greene, to the allied arms, to the corporation of Richmond, to the friends of freedom throughout the world, to the immortal memory of those illustrious heroes, who have fallen

Residents of Henrico County serving as noncommissioned officers or privates, 1780–81

Name	Age	Occupation	Entered as	Date entered	Period of Enlistment
Allen, Isham	17	planter	enlisted	8/20/80	—
Alley, David	45	planter	enlisted	8/30/80	18 months[1]
Campin, William	27	founder	substitute	4/—/81	the war
Childress, Merideth	19	planter	enlisted	9/7/78	3 years
Eubank, James	29	farmer	enlisted	5/2/81	18 months
Eubank, Thomas	31	farmer	drafted	4/12/81	18 months[2]
Fitsgarel, George	25	—	drafted	12/—/80 [?]	18 months
Fitzgrel, George	40	planter	enlisted	8/30/80	18 months
Franklin, James	25	farmer	enlisted	11/1/77	3 years
Fuzzel, John	19	farmer	enlisted	2/19/79	25 months[3]
Garrison, John[4]	25	planter	enlisted	8/15/80	18 months
Green, Isaac	24	farmer	enlisted	11/—/77	3 years[5]
Green, William[4]	19	farmer	enlisted	8/7/79	18 months
Grinstead, John	20	farmer	drafted	4/13/81	18 months
Himas, William	17	planter	substitute	3/13/81	18 months
Killey, William	22	farmer	enlisted	11/1/77	3 years
Killey, William	28	bricklayer	substitute	3/22/—	18 months
King, Phillip	22	hatter	substitute	3/24/81	to 2/10/82
Lawrence, Absalom	19	—	drafted	4/6/81	18 months
Plowman, Robert	60	farmer	enlisted	4/75; 3/81	18 months (each enlistment)

Pruett, Ambrose	40	C. [cabinet?] maker	enlisted	8/11/80	18 months
Radford, ———	25	carpenter	drafted	8/—/80[?]	—
Rogers, Bolin[4]	15	farmer	enlisted	9/15/80	the war
Rogers, Theodorick	21	planter	enlisted	8/8/78	the war
Rogers, Thomas	18	planter	enlisted	2/19/79	18 months
Sanders, John[6]	16	farmer	substitute	4/16/81	18 months
Scott, Littleberry[6]	18	farmer	substitute	3/28/81	the war
Scott, Thomas	18	planter	enlisted	7/11/78	the war
Sharp, John	25	blacksmith	enlisted	9/14/80	18 months[7]
Sharp, Richard	—	planter	enlisted	9/18/80	18 months
Sharplin, James	21	blacksmith	enlisted	8/30/80	18 months[8]
Shepperd, William[6]	19	farmer	drafted	4/13/81	18 months
Thomas, John	21	planter	substitute	3/24/81	18 months
Twines [?] John[4]	18	planter	substitute	9/—/80	18 months
Williams, Benjamin[9]	21	S. [shoe?] maker	substitute	4/13/81	18 months
Williams, Robin[6]	17	cooper	substitute	3/24/81	18 months
———, John	17	farmer	enlisted	5/18/80	the war
[name illegible]	18	carpenter	substitute	4/17/81	18 months

[1] Deserted and retaken.
[2] Discharged before end of term.
[3] Deserted before end of term.
[4] Indicated on rolls as resident of Richmond.
[5] Time expired and discharged.
[6] Mustered at Powhatan Court House—Henrico man.
[7] Deserted from under guard; was once wagon master in Virginia Line.
[8] Deserted from Chesterfield Court House, Dec. 1780; right forefinger missing to first joint.
[9] Mustered at Carter's Ferry—Henrico man.

in the defence of their country, and to the glorious anniversary of the 4th of July.

Later in July the Richmond Common Hall gave its own "elegant entertainment to the citizens, at which were present . . . the Governor, the Officers of State, and a numerous company of Gentlemen. . . . "

For Richmond, 1783 was a time of celebration. John Marshall wrote a friend in February of attending a dancing assembly held every fortnight in Richmond. He described the most recent in this way: "The last was a brilliant one; twas on the Generals birthnight. Never did I see such a collection of handsome ladies. I do not belive that Versailles or St. James's ever displayed so much beauty." On July 4, 1783, thirteen discharges of cannon were fired at the rising of the sun, at twelve o'clock noon, and at sunset. A Richmond newspaper reported: "Yesterday being the glorious Anniversary of Independence was celebrated here with utmost demonstrations of joy."

Dr. Johann David Schoepf, who commented on everything he saw, described the culminating celebration of 1783 as itself a triumph of democratic equality:

News of the definitive treaty just arrived in America was the occasion at Richmond of illuminations, fire-works, banquetings, and finally, a ball, at which the honor of the first dance fell by lot to the very honorable daughter of a very honorable shoemaker. That the distinction should have been awarded by lot was the cause of great displeasure to the ladies of the Governor's family and his relatives, and the incident was the subject of every conversation the next day, but the unanimous opinion was that the lot should be valid as against any claims of rank, and that no exception to the generally allowed equality should be granted even the fair sex beyond that due personal merit and accomplishment.

Bibliography

Index

Bibliography

Among the most valuable sources of information on life in Richmond during the Revolution are the local archives. Records of Richmond Common Hall, Richmond Hustings Court, and the Henrico County Court were used extensively. These records are in the Virginia State Library and the City of Richmond Courts Building. Richmond city records are complete from the city's founding in 1782. Henrico County records were destroyed by the British in 1781 and were afterwards only partially reconstructed for the period 1775–81, upon affidavits pertaining to property rights.

The handwritten notes of Edward V. Valentine, preserved in the Valentine Museum, Richmond, have aided in the identification and location of early buildings in Richmond, particularly taverns.

Williamsburg and Richmond newspapers for 1775–83 provide valuable information on social and economic life, especially through advertisements. Newspaper issues during the war years were irregular. For the Williamsburg newspapers, a helpful guide has been Lester Cappon and Stella F. Duff, *Virginia Gazette Index, 1736–1780* (2 vols. [Williamsburg, 1950]).

Douglas Southall Freeman observed in his biography of Washington that the Steuben Papers, the single most valuable record of military activities in Virginia during the British invasion, were still waiting use by historians of Virginia. This book is the first to use extensively the Steuben Papers as a source of Virginia history. The collection, in microfilm, is readily available through interlibrary loan from the New-York Historical Society.

From the huge collection of the Executive Papers at the Virginia State Library, a number of the letters to and from the governors of Virginia that pertain to the period of this study have already appeared in *The Papers of Thomas Jefferson* (ed. Boyd) and in the *Official Letters of the Governors* (ed. McIlwaine).

But the collection has a tremendous number of letters and reports to the Virginia Executive that have not been published. The Executive Papers collection has been an important source, both for the day-to-day account of the Virginia civil and military government in Richmond and for the social and personal history. Lesser holdings of the Virginia State Library (but also significant for this study), are such collections as the Executive Communications, Legislative Petitions, personal correspondence, and business ledgers.

One important source for Virginia history—not available at the time of writing of this book, but which should be brought to the attention of the reader—is the Allyn K. Ford Collection at the Minnesota Historical Society. The collection, used extensively by Freeman, was in private hands for a long time and seemed for a while to have vanished. After the death of Ford, however, the Minnesota Historical Society eventually acquired it from the estate and has recently issued it in a microfilm edition. Although this material is somewhat peripheral to the history of Richmond during the Revolution, the collection does contain letters by all prominent Virginians and by many not so well known.

Much of the literature relating to Richmond during the Revolution is in the form of typewritten theses and other unpublished monographs. Wirt Armistead Cate's three-volume history of Richmond, though most deserving, has never appeared in published form. Although it slights the revolutionary period and omits the military aspects, it was an invaluable aid. The authors express gratitude to Mr. Cate, who now resides in Tennessee, for permission to consult this manuscript at the Valentine Museum. Numerous academic theses were used, and those that were substantially productive are included in the bibliography. Most of the older theses were obtained through interlibrary loan; others were used at the Library of Congress, and several were purchased from University Microfilms, Ann Arbor, Michigan. Most rewarding of the theses were Konigsberg's "Edward Carrington" and McMurran's "The Virginia Claims of William Cuninghame and Company." For a substantially complete listing of theses on Virginia history, see Richard R. Duncan and Dorothy M. Brown, "Theses and Dissertations on Virginia History," in *The Virginia Magazine of*

History and Biography 79 (1971):55–109, and a supplement by the same compilers in vol. 83 (1975), pp. 346–67.

The published accounts of visitors to the city prior to or during the Revolution are a major source of information. The most important of these visitors—most of whom either were serving with the British or American armies or had some military connection at one time or another—include Thomas Anburey, the marquis de Chastellux, Johann David Schoepf, J. D. F. Smyth, Ebenezer Wild, Joseph Feltman, and John Graves Simcoe. Although he wrote after the war, Daniel Trabue, an enlisted man of Chesterfield County, gives the most vivid feeling and impressions of what it was like to live through the British invasions in the Richmond area. Betsy Ambler, a Richmond resident, similarly tells in detail of the flight of a Richmond family from the British invaders. The personal correspondence of Virginians of the time also contains occasional glimpses of the city and its life.

Archival publications of other states, which chiefly deal with their military units in the Richmond area, afford some significant items.

Published special and general studies have contributed material aiding interpretative analysis and some important data.

The original manuscript of this book contains complete annotation. Although the expository footnote was avoided, in some instances the notes also evaluated the accuracy of a particular source or of conflicting eyewitness accounts. The annotation may be viewed at the Richmond Independence Bicentennial Commission.

In the bibliographical citations that follow, *The Virginia Magazine of History and Biography* is abbreviated *VMHB; The William and Mary Quarterly,* as *WMQ.* Manuscripts from other collections that are also available on microfilm at the Virginia State Library are indicated in the bibliography by an asterisk.

I. Manuscripts

American Philosophical Society, Philadelphia

Correspondence of General George Weedon
Correspondence of General Nathanael Greene, 1777–80
Sol Feinstone Revolutionary War Collection

City of Richmond Courts Building

Richmond Husting Court Order Book, Vol. 1, 1782–87

Library of Congress

*Diary of Robert Honeyman, M.D., January 2, 1776–March 11, 1782
State of the Loyalists in Virginia Miscellaneous Documents (includes Gov. William Franklin's letter to Lord Germain, November 6, 1781)

*Washington Papers

    Series 3. Varick transcripts—Washington's Revolutionary War Correspondence: subseries B—Continental and State military Personnel; subseries C—Civil Officials and Citizens
    Series 4. General Correspondence

National Archives

Miscellaneous Revolutionary War Records
    Letters Received by Timothy Pickering, 1781
    Records, Commissioner of Accounts
    Records of Disbursements
Revolutionary War Records Relating to Virginia, U.S. War Department

*Papers of the Continental Congress

    Letters Addressed to Congress
    Letters and Papers Relating to the Quarter Master Department, 1777–84
    Letters of Nathanael Greene
    Miscellaneous
    Virginia State Papers

New-York Historical Society

Benedict Arnold Papers
Papers of General Horatio Gates
Papers of Major General Baron von Steuben

New York Public Library

American Loyalists Transcript of the Manuscript Books and Papers of the Commission of Enquiry into the Losses and Services of the American Loyalists . . . Preserved amongst the Audit Office Records in the Public Record Office of England, 1783–90, vols. 27, 32, 58, and 59

Public Record Office, Great Britain (available through Virginia Records Project, VSL)

*Audit Office: Loyalist Claims
*Cornwallis Papers
*Customs, vol. 14
*Special Agents Reports on Claims, 1784–85
*State of the Loyalists in Virginia: transcripts, Colonial Office (Great Britain)
*Treasury Out-Letters

University of Virginia

*The Lee Family Papers

Valentine Museum

Cowley's Tavern File
Formicola's Tavern File
Galt's City Tavern File
Valentine's Notes: Hotels and Taverns

Virginia Historical Society

Adams Family Papers (Richard and Thomas)
Henry Banks Papers
Westover Papers

Virginia State Library (Many of the collections listed below are available in photoduplicated form.)

Account of Property Taken by the British in Virginia Belonging to Mitchell and Gamble in Losses caused by the British
Capitol Square Data: Virginia Documents Relating to the Capitol, typescripts

Commercial Agent: Ledger, August 1780–January 1782
                    Day Book, March 16, 1781–July 17, 1782
                    Journal, February 1781–November 1782
                    Ledger, February 1781–November 1782
                    Day Book, July 18–December 18, 1782
Commissioner of the Navy Journal, July 21–December 19, 1780
Committee of Safety:Accounts, 1775–76
                    Ledger
                    Papers
Dabney-Jackson Collection, photostats
Executive Communications, 1776–83
Executive Letter Books, 1776–83
Executive Papers, 1776–83
Henrico County Minutes of the Monthly Meeting of the Quakers, 1780–83
Henrico County Deed and Will Book, vol. 1, 1781–85; vol. 2, 1785–88
Henrico Court Order Book, vol. 1, 1781–84
Ledger Book, Tobacco Warehouses, 1781
Legislative Petitions: Henrico County, 1778–85
                         Hanover County, 1776–86
                         Chesterfield County, 1776–83
                         Richmond City, 1776–87
                         Religion, 1774–1802
Letters of Captain Samuel Jones, Asst. QMG
Losses caused by the British File
Lt. Col. Christian Febiger Letter Books, 1779–80 and 1780–82, transcripts
Minutes of the [Virginia] Board of Trade, 1779–80
Miscellaneous Revolutionary War Collection
Papers of the Commissioners and Quarter Master at Point of Fork and Richmond, 1783–87
Proceedings of Commissioners Respecting the Records of the Henrico Court Destroyed by the British, 1774–82
Proceedings of the Directors of the Public Buildings, July 17, 1780, typescript
Public Store, Richmond: Account Book, November 5, 1782–May 21, 1783, and Receipt Book, Nov. 5, 1782–July 22, 1783
Public Store, Richmond: Ledger, March 16, 1781–December 18, 1782

Public Store, Williamsburg: Ledger Book, October 12, 1775– October 17, 1776

Registers of Noncommissioned Officers and Privates: Chesterfield Court House; Powhatan Court House; Carter's Ferry; Albemarle Old Court House; Cumberland Old Court House; and Winchester Barracks—1777–83

Revolutionary Navy Records

Richmond City Hustings Deeds, no. 1, 1782–92

Richmond Common Hall Records, vol. 1, 1782–92

Size-Roll of Troops Join'd at Chesterfield Court House since September 12, 1780

State Agency Papers, 1776–79

Virginia Conventions, 1775–76:   Petitions
                                  Resolutions
                                  Miscellaneous Papers

Virginia Land Office: Revolution—Military Bounty Warrants

Vouchers of the Rope Factory

War Book no. 1: Revolutionary Officers, Continental and State Lines and Navy

War Office Letter Book, 1779–82

Westham Public Foundry: John Reveley's Accounts, 1779–80

Westham Public Foundry Ledger, 1776–79, 1779–81

II.   Newspapers

The Virginia Gazette. (Pinkney, pub.) Williamsburg, 1775–76.

The Virginia Gazette. (Purdie, pub.) Williamsburg, 1775–78.

The Virginia Gazette. (Dixon and Hunter, pubs.) Williamsburg, 1775–78.

The Virginia Gazette. (Dixon and Nicolson, pubs.) Williamsburg, 1779–80.

The Virginia Gazette. (Dixon and Nicolson, pubs.) Richmond, 1780–81.

The Virginia Gazette, or, the American Advertiser. (Hayes, pub.) Richmond, 1781–84.

The Virginia Gazette, and Weekly Advertiser. (Nicolson and Prentis, pubs.) Richmond, 1782.

The Virginia Gazette or the Independent Chronicle. (Dixon and Holt, pubs.) Richmond, 1783.

III.   Theses and Other Unpublished Works

Armentrout, Mary T. "A Political Study of Virginia Finance, 1781–89." Ph.D. diss., University of Virginia, 1934.

Brown, Fred M. "Tobacco Trade in Virginia during the Revolution." M.A. thesis, University of Virginia, 1934.

Cate, Wirt Armistead. "History of Richmond, Virginia." 3 vols. Valentine Museum, Richmond, Va., n.d. Typescript.

Cox, Elbert. "The Virginia Phase of the Origin of the First Continental Congress." M.A. thesis, University of Virginia, 1931.

Curtis, George M. "The Virginia Courts During the Revolution." Ph.D. diss., University of Wisconsin, 1970.

DuVal, Miles P., Jr. "Samuel DuVal: Torchbearer of Liberty." Dedicatory address at unveiling of tablet for Samuel DuVal at the St. John's Church, Richmond, April 5, 1970. Typescript.

Frick, Bertha M. "A History of Printing in Virginia, 1780–83, with a list of Virginia Imprints for That Period." M.S. thesis, Columbia University, 1933.

Goodwin, Mary R. M. "Clothing and Accoutrements of the Officers of the Virginia Forces, 1775–80: From the Record of the Public Store at Williamsburg." Colonial Williamsburg, 1962. Typescript.

Guy, John Ansley. "Institutional Reforms in Virginia, 1775–1800." M.A. thesis, Duke University, 1939.

Hatch, Charles E. "Colonel William Aylett: A Revolutionary Merchant of Virginia." M.A. thesis, University of Virginia, 1936.

Hester, Mary F. "The Public Career of John Harvie." M.A. thesis, University of Virginia, 1938.

Hill, Tucker H. "A History of St. John's Church and the Domestic Architecture Which Surrounded It, 1741–1861." M.A. thesis, University of Virginia, 1967.

Hilldrup, Robert L. "The Virginia Convention of 1776: A Study in Revolutionary Politics." Ph.D. diss., University of Virginia, 1935.

Hosier, James W., III. "Travellers' Comments on Virginia Taverns, Ordinaries, and Other Accomodations from 1750 to 1812." M.A. thesis, University of Richmond, 1964.

Johnson, Robert. "Government Regulation of Business Enterprise in Virginia, 1750–1820." Ph.D. diss., University of Minnesota, 1958.

Knepper, George W. "The Convention Army, 1777–83." Ph.D. diss., University of Michigan, 1954.

Konigsberg, Charles. "Edward Carrington, 1748–1810, Child of the Revolution: A Study of the Public Man in Young America." Ph.D. diss., Princeton University, 1966.

McMurran, Richard E. "The Virginia Claims of William Cuninghame and Company, 1784–1811." M.A. thesis, University of Alabama, 1965.

Rachal, William M. E. "Archibald Cary and the Revolution in Virginia." M.A. thesis, University of Virginia, 1938. (Includes correspondence of Cary, pp. 62–126.)

Rich, Myra L. "The Experimental Years: Virginia, 1781–89." Ph.D. diss., Yale University, 1966.

Sellers, John R. "The Virginia Continental Line, 1775–80." Ph.D. diss., Tulane University, 1968.

Smith, Glenn Curtis. "Pamphleteers and the American Revolution in Virginia, 1752–76." Ph.D. diss., University of Virginia, 1937.

Stoutamire, Albert L. "A History of Music in Richmond, Virginia, from 1742 to 1865." Ph.D. diss., Florida State University, 1960.

Sullivan, Mary. "The Association in Virginia, 1774–76." M.A. thesis, University of Virginia, 1963.

Teeter, Sara E. "Benjamin Harrison, Governor of Virginia, 1781–84." M.A. thesis, University of Richmond, 1963.

IV.   Contemporary Sources in Published Form

[Ambler, Eliza J.] "Letter of Eliza J. Ambler to Mrs. Dudley." *VMHB* 38 (1930):167–69.

Anburey, Thomas. *Travels Through the Interior Parts of America, in a Series of Letters.* Vol. 2, London, 1791.

Andrews, Robert. *The Virginia Almanack.* Richmond, 1781–83.

"An Old Virginia Correspondence." *The Atlantic Monthly* 84 (1889):535–49.

"Army Supplies in the Revolution." *VMHB* 4 (1897):387–400.

Bannister, John. "John Bannister to Elisha Tupper." *VMHB* 28 (1920):266–73.

—. "Letter from John Banister [of Battersea near Petersburg]." *VMHB* 28 (1920):266–73.

Barnhart, John D., ed. *Henry Hamilton and George Rogers Clark in the American Revolution, with the Unpublished Journal of Lieut. Gov. Henry Hamilton.* Crawfordsville, Ind., 1951.

[Baurmeister, Carl L.] *Revolution in America: Confidential Letters and Journals, 1776–1784, of Adjutant General Major Baurmeister of the Hessian Forces.* Translated and edited by Bernhard A. Uhlendorf. New Brunswick, N.J., 1957.

Blanchard, Claude. *The Journal of Claude Blanchard.* Edited by William Duane and Thomas Balch. Albany, 1876.

Bland, Theodorick. *The Bland Papers: Being a Selection from the Manuscripts of Colonel Theodorick Bland of Prince George County.* Edited by Charles Campbell. 2 vols. Petersburg, Va., 1840, 1843.

Brenaman, J. N., ed. *A History of Virginia Conventions.* Richmond, 1902.

Brooke, Francis T. *Narrative of My Life: For My Family.* Richmond, 1849.

Burnaby, Andrew. *Travels through the Middle Settlements in North American in the Years 1759 and 1760.* London, 1775.

Burnett, Edmund C., ed. *Letters of Members of the Continental Congress.* 8 vols. Washington, D.C., 1921–36.

Call, Daniel, ed. *Reports of Cases Argued and Decided in the Court of Appeals of Virginia.* Vol. 4. Richmond, 1833.

Canby, Courtlandt, ed. "Robert Munford: *The Patriots.*" *WMQ*, 3d ser. 6 (1949):437–503.

Chastellux, marquis de. *Travels in North America in the Years 1780, 1781, and 1782.* 2 vols. London, 1787.

Clark, Walter, ed. *The State Records of North Carolina.* Vol. 11 (Winston, N.C., 1895) and Vol. 19 (Goldsboro, N.C., 1901).

Cleggett, David A. H., ed. "Hector McAlester's Plans for the Subjugation of Virginia, [late] 1780." *VMHB* 82 (1974):75–83.

[Clinton, Sir Henry.] *The American Rebellion: Sir Henry Clinton, Narrative of His Campaigns, 1778–82.* Edited by William B. Willcox. New Haven, 1954.

Coke, Daniel Parker. *The Royal Commission on the Losses and Services of American Loyalists, 1783–85: Being the Notes of Mr.*

Daniel Parker Coke, M.P., One of the Commissioners during that Period. Edited by Hugh E. Egerton. 1915. Reprint. New York, 1969.

Cornwallis, Charles. *Correspondence of Charles, First Marquis Cornwallis.* Edited by Charles Ross. Vol. 1. London, 1859.

"Correspondence in 1774 and 1775 Between a Committee of the Town of Boston and Contributors of Donations for the Relief of the Sufferers by the Boston Port Bill." *Collections of the Massachusetts Historical Society.*" 4th ser., 4:1–278. Boston, 1858.

[Davis, John.] "The Yorktown Campaign: Journal of Captain John Davis of the Pennsylvania Line." *PMHB* 5 (1881):290–310.

Denny, William H., ed. "Military Journal of Major Ebenezer Denny." *Memoirs of the Historical Society of Pennsylvania* 7 (1860):205–409.

"Extract of Brigadier-General Arnold's Letter to Sir Henry Clinton, May 12, 1781, Petersburgh." *WMQ*, 2d ser. 12 (1932):187–89.

[Feltman, William.] *The Journal of Lieut. William Feltman of the First Pennsylvania Regiment, 1781–82.* Philadelphia, 1853.

Force, Peter, ed. *American Archives: A Documentary History of the English Colonies in North America from March 7, 1774, to the Declaration of Independence.* 4th ser., vols. 1–6 (1837–46); 5th ser., vols. 1–3 (1848–53). Washington, D.C.

Hamilton, Alexander. *The Papers of Alexander Hamilton.* Edited by Harold C. Syrett and Jacob E. Cooke. Vol. 2. New York, 1961.

Hening, William W., ed. *The Statutes at Large, Being a Collection of All the Laws of Virginia.* Vols. 8–40. Richmond, 1821–22.

Henry, William Wirt., ed. *Patrick Henry: Life, Correspondence, and Speeches.* 3 vols. New York, 1891.

Hillman, Benjamin J., ed. *Executive Journals of the Council of Colonial Virginia.* Vol. 6 (1754–75). Richmond, 1966.

Jefferson, Thomas. *Notes on the State of Virginia* (1782). Edited by William Peden. Chapel Hill, N.C., 1955.

———. *The Papers of Thomas Jefferson.* Edited by Julian P. Boyd. Vol. 1–6. Princeton, N.J., 1950–1952.

Jones, Joseph. *Letters of Joseph Jones of Virginia, 1777–1787.* Edited by Worthington C. Ford. 1889. Reprinted New York, 1971.

Journals of the Council of the State of Virginia.
  Vols. 1–2. Edited by H. R. McIlwaine, Richmond, 1931–32.
  Vol. 3. Edited by Wilmer L. Hall, Richmond, 1952.
  Vol. 4. Edited by George H. Reese, Richmond, 1967.
Journals of the House of Delegates of Virginia.
  1776 Session. Richmond, 1828.
  May 5, 1777, and subsequent sessions through 1786, published individually but bound in 2 vols. Richmond, 1827–28.
  March 1781 Session. *Bulletin of the VSL,* Vol. 17, no. 1., (January 1928).
Journals of the Senate of the Commonwealth of Virginia.
  Session: October 7, 1776. Williamsburg, 1776.
          May 4, 1778. Williamsburg, 1778.
          October 5, 1778. Richmond, 1828.
          October 4, 1779. Richmond, 1828.
          May 3, 1779. Richmond, 1828.
          October 20, 1783. Richmond, 1783.
Kennedy, John P., ed. *Journals of the House of Burgesses of Virginia 1773–76, Including the Records of the Committee of Correspondence.* Richmond, 1905.
Lafayette, marquis de. *Lafayette in America Day by Day* [chronology and extracts of Lafayette's letters].
  Compiled by J. Bennett Nolan. Baltimore, 1934.
  ———. *Lafayette in Virginia: Unpublished Letters from the Original Manuscripts in the Virginia State Library and the Library of Congress.* Edited by Gilbert Chinard. Baltimore, 1928.
  ———. "Letters from Lafayette to Luzerne, 1780–82." Edited by Waldo G. Leland and Edmund C. Burnett. *American Historical Review* 20 (1915):341–76, 577–612. (Assistance in translation by Mrs. W. H. Pursley of Richmond.)
  ———. "Letters of Lafayette." *VMHB* 5 (1898): 374–83.
  ———. *Memoirs of the Marquis de La Fayette . . . together with His Tour through the United States.* Edited by Frederick Butler, Wethersfield, Conn., 1825.
The [Charles]*Lee Papers.* Collections of the New-York Historical Society, vols. 4–7. New York, 1871–74.
Lee, Richard Henry. *The Letters of Richard Henry Lee.* Edited by James C. Ballagh. 2 vols. New York, 1911, 1914.
"Letters to Jefferson from Archibald Cary and Robert Gamble." *WMQ,* 2d ser. 6 (1926):122–30.

"Letters to Thomas Adams." *VMHB* 5 (1898):374–83 and 6 (1899):30–32.

McClellan, Capt. Joseph. "Journal [of the Pennsylvania Line], May–June 1781." *Pennsylvania Archives,* 2d ser. 11 (Harrisburg, Pa., 1895):708–10.

McIlwaine, H. R., ed. *Official Letters of the Governors of the State of Virginia.* 3 vols. (1776–83). Richmond, 1926–29.

Madison, James. *The Papers of James Madison.* Edited by William T. Hutchinson and William M. E. Rachal. Vols. 1–6. Chicago, 1962–69.

Marshall, John. *The Papers of John Marshall.* Edited by Herbert A. Johnson. Vol. 1. Chapel Hill, N.C., 1974.

Mason, George. *The Papers of George Mason, 1725–1792.* Edited by Robert A. Rutland. Vols. 1, 2. Chapel Hill, N.C., 1970.

Mason, Frances Norton, ed. *John Norton & Sons, Merchants of London and Virginia, Being the Papers from Their Counting House for the Years 1750 to 1795.* Richmond, 1937.

Memoirs of a Monticello Slave, as dictated to Charles Campbell by Isaac. In *Jefferson at Monticello,* edited by James Bear. Charlottesville, Va., 1967. (Isaac's narrative was recorded in 1847.)

Moore, J. Staunton, ed. *Henrico Parish and Old St. John's Church, Richmond, Virginia, 1611–1904.* Richmond, 1904. Includes: Burton, Lewis W., ed., "Annals of Henrico Parish . . . and . . . St. John's Church, 1611–1904"; Brock, R. A., ed., "The Vestry Book of Henrico Parish, Virginia, 1730–73, with Notes and Appendix"; and Moore, J. Staunton, ed., "Inscriptions upon the Tombstones."

Morrison, Alfred J., ed. *Travels in Virginia in Revolutionary Times.* Lynchburg, Va., 1922.

Muster and Pay Rolls of the War of the Revolution, 1775–83, Vol. 2. Vol. 68 of the *Collections of the New-York Historical Society.* New York, 1916.

Ordinances of the Corporation of the City of Richmond and the Acts of Assembly Relating Thereto. Richmond, 1831.

Palmer, W. P., et al., eds. *Calendar of Virginia State Papers and Other Manuscripts Preserved in the Capitol at Richmond.* Vol. 1, Richmond, 1875.

Powell, Robert C. *A Biographical Sketch of Col. Leven Powell, Including His Correspondence during the Revolutionary War.* Alexandria, Va., 1877.

"Preston Papers." *VMHB* 26 (1918):363–79; 27 (1919):42–49, 157–66, 309–25; 28 (1920):109–16, 241–46, 346–52; 29 (1921):29–35.

Proceedings of the Convention of Delegates for the Countries and Corporations in the Colony of Virginia . . . July 17, 1775. Richmond, 1816.

Proceedings of the Convention of Delegates Held at the Town of Richmond, Friday, December 1, 1775, and Afterwards by Adjournment in the City of Williamsburg. Richmond, 1816.

Proceedings of the Convention of Delegates Held at the Capitol . . . May 6, 1776. Richmond, 1816.

Randolph, Edmund. *History of Virginia* [written 1809–13]. Edited by Arthur H. Shaffer, *Virginia Historical Society Documents,* vol. 9. Charlottesville, Va., 1970.

Reed, William B., ed. *Life and Correspondence of Joseph Reed.* 2 vols. Philadelphia, 1847.

Report on the Manuscripts of Mrs. Stopford-Sackville of Drayton House, Northamptonshire. Vol. 2. Hereford, Eng., 1910.

[Riedesel, Baron Friedrich Adolph von.] *Memoirs and Letters and Journals of Major General Riedesel during His Residence in America.* Translated and edited by William L. Stone. Vol. 2. Albany, 1868.

[Riedesel, Baroness von.] *Baroness von Riedesel and the American Revolution: Journal and Correspondence of a Tour of Duty, 1776–83.* Translated and edited by Marvin L. Brown, Jr. Chapel Hill, N.C., 1965.

Saffell, W. T. R., ed. *Records of the Revolutionary War. . . .* New York, 1858.

St. Clair, Arthur. *The St. Clair Papers: The Life and Public Services of Arthur St. Clair, . . . with his Correspondence and Other Papers.* Edited by William H. Smith. Vol. 1. Cincinnati, 1882.

Schoepf, Johann David. *Travels in the Confederation* [1783–84]. Translated and edited by Alfred J. Morrison. Vol. 2. Reprint. New York, 1968.

Simcoe, Lt. Col. John Graves. *A Journal of the Operations of The Queen's Rangers from the End of the Year 1777 to the Conclusion of the Late American War.* 1787. Reprint. New York, 1844.

Smyth, J. F. D. *A Tour in the United States of America.* London, 1784.

Stevens, Benjamin F., ed. *The Campaign in Virginia: An Exact Reprint of Six Rare Pamphlets on the Clinton-Cornwallis Controversy, with . . . Unpublished Manuscript Notes by Sir Henry Clinton.* 2 vols. London, 1888.

Tarleton, Lt. Col. Banastre. *A History of the Campaigns of 1780 and 1781 in the Southern Provinces of North America.* London, 1787. Reprint. London, 1967.

Thacher, James. *Military Journal of the American Revolution.* Hartford, Conn., 1862.

[Trabue, Daniel.] "The Journal of Colonel Daniel Trabue." In *Colonial Men and Times,* edited by Lillie D. V. Harper, pp. 3–156. Philadelphia, 1916.

Virginia State Library Leaflets.

No. 6. *"Address* [Henrico County] . . . to . . . Representatives [Virginia Convention, Williamsburg], July 15, 1774." Richmond, October 1904.

No. 7. "Committee of Safety . . . [Resolution of Convention], August 1775." Richmond, November 1904.

Washington, George. *The Diaries of George Washington.* Edited by John C. Fitzpatrick. Vol. 2. Boston, 1925.

———. *The Writings of George Washington.* Edited by John C. Fitzpatrick. 39 vols. Washington, D.C., 1931–44.

[Wild, Ebenezer.] "Journal of Ebenezer Wild." *Proceedings of the Mass. Hist. Society,* 2d ser. 6 (1890):78–160.

Willcox, William B., ed. *The American Rebellion: Sir Henry Clinton, Narrative of his Campaigns, 1778–82.* New Haven, 1954.

V.   Secondary Works and Registers

Alden, John R. *The South in the Revolution, 1763–1789.* A History of the South, Edited by W. H. Stephenson and E. M. Coulter, vol. 3. Baton Rouge, La., 1957.

Alexander, Arthur J. "Desertion and Its Punishment in Revolutionary Virginia." *WMQ,* 3d ser. 3 (1946):383–97.

Allen, Sarah C. *Our Children's Ancestry.* Atlanta, 1935.

Baker, Leonard. *John Marshall: A Life in Law.* New York, 1974.

Bass, Robert D. *The Green Dragoon: The Lives of Banastre Tarleton and Mary Robinson.* New York, 1957.

Beeman, Richard R. *Patrick Henry: A Biography.* New York, 1974.

Berg, Fred A. *Encyclopedia of Continental Army Units: Battalions, Regiments, and Independent Corps.* Harrisburg, Pa., 1972.

Berkeley, Edmund, and Berkeley, Dorothy S. *John Beckley, Zealous Partisan in a Nation Divided.* Philadelphia, 1973.

Berkin, Carol. "The Women of the American Revolution." *The American Way* (May 1974), pp. 26–31.

Berry, Thomas S. "The Rise of Flour Milling In Richmond." *VMHB* 78 (1970):387–408.

Beveridge, Albert J. *The Life of John Marshall.* Vol. 1. New York, 1916.

Blanton, Wyndham B. *Medicine in Virginia in the Eighteenth Century.* Richmond, 1931.

Boatner, Mark M. *Encyclopedia of the American Revolution.* New York, 1966.

Bowman, Allen. *The Morale of the American Revolutionary Army.* 1943. Reprint. Port Washington, N.Y., 1964.

Bowman, Larry G. "The Scarcity of Salt in Virginia during the American Revolution." *VMHB* 77 (1969):464–72.

Bridenbaugh, Carl. *Cities in Revolt: Urban Life in America, 1743–1776.* New York, 1964.

Brock, Robert K. *Archibald Cary of Ampthill.* Richmond, 1937.

Brodie, Fawn M. *Thomas Jefferson: An Intimate History.* New York, 1974.

Brown, Alexander. *The Cabells and their Kin.* 1895. 2d ed. Richmond, 1939.

Brown, Robert E., and Brown, B. Katherine. *Virginia 1705–1786: Democracy or Aristocracy?* East Lansing, Mich., 1964.

Brown, Wallace. *The Good Americans: The Loyalists in the American Revolution.* New York, 1969.

———. *The King's Friends: The Composition and Motives of the American Loyalists Claimants.* Providence, R.I., 1965.

Bruce, Kathleen. *Virginia Iron Manufacture in the Slave Era.* New York, 1931.

Brumbaugh, Gaius M. *Revolutionary War Records* [Register]. Vol. 1, *Virginia.* Washington, D.C., 1936.

Brydon, George M. "The Clergy of the Established Church in Virginia and the Revolution." *VMHB* 61 (1943):11–23, 123–43, 231–43, 297–309.

————. *Virginia's Mother Church and the Political Conditions under Which It Grew.* 2 vols. Richmond and Philadelphia, 1947–52.

Burgess, Louis D. *Virginia Soldiers of 1776.* 3 vols. Richmond, 1927–29.

Burk, John Daly. *History of Virginia, from Its First Settlement to the Commencement of the Revolution.* Vols. 3, 4. Vol. 4 continued by Skeleton Jones and Louis H. Girardin. Petersburg, Va., 1805, 1816.

Callahan, North. *Flight from the Republic: The Tories of the American Revolution.* Indianapolis, 1967.

Campbell, Norine D. *Patrick Henry: Patriot and Statesman.* New York, 1969.

Carrington, Henry B. *Battles of the American Revolution, 1775–81.* New York, 1876.

————. "Lafayette's Virginia Campaign, 1781." *Magazine of American History* 6 (1881):340–52. (Includes Carrington's map of Lafayette's Virginia campaigns—see fig. 21.)

Carson, Jane. *Colonial Virginians at Play.* Williamsburg, Va., 1965.

————. *James Innes and His Brothers of the F. H. C.* Williamsburg, 1965.

Chapin, Bradley. "Colonial and Revolutionary Origins of the American Law of Treason." *WMQ*, 3d ser. 17 (1960):3–21.

Christian, W. Asbury. *Richmond, Her Past and Present.* Richmond, 1912.

Clark, Thomas D. *Travels in the Old South: A Bibliography.* Vol. 2. Norman, Okla., 1956.

Clarkin, William. *Serene Patriot: A Life of George Wythe.* New York, 1970.

Coleman, Charles W. "The County Committees of 1774–75 in Virginia." *WMQ*, 1st ser. 5 (1897):94–106, 245–55.

Cometti, Elizabeth. "Depredations in Virginia during the Revolution." In *The Old Dominion: Essays for Thomas Perkins Abernathy*, edited by Darrett B. Rutman, pp. 135–51. Charlottesville, Va., 1964.

Cunningham, Noble E., Jr. "John Beckley: An Early American Party Manager." *WMQ*, 3d ser. 13 (1956):40–52.

Dabney, Charles W. "Colonel Charles Dabney of the Revolution: His Service as Soldier and Citizen." *VMHB* 51 (1943):186–99.

Dabney, William M. *After Saratoga: The Story of the Convention Army.* Albuquerque, N. Mex., 1954.

Davis, Burke. *The Campaign that Won America: The Story of Yorktown.* New York, 1970.

Dawson, Henry P. *Battles of the United States by Sea and Land.* Vol. 1. New York. 1858.

Dew, Charles B. "David Ross and the Oxford Iron Works: A Study of Industrial Slavery in the Early Nineteenth Century South." *WMQ,* 3d ser. 31 (1974):189–224.

Dodd, William E. "Virginia Takes the Road to Revolution." In *The Spirit of '76 and Other Essays,* edited by Carl Becker, et al., pp. 99–132. Washington, D.C., 1927.

Dowdey, Clifford. *The Great Plantation: A Profile of Berkeley Hundred and Plantation, Virginia, From Jamestown to Appomattox.* Berkeley Plantation, Charles City, Va., 1957.

Duff, Stella. "The Case Against the King: The *Virginia Gazettes* Indict George III." WMQ, 3d ser. 6 (1949):383–97.

Dumbauld, Edward. *Thomas Jefferson: American Tourist.* Norman, Okla., 1946.

Duncan, Louis. *Medical Men in the American Revolution, 1775–83.* Carlisle Barracks, Pa., 1931.

Eckenrode, H. J. *The Randolphs.* Indianapolis, 1946.

——. *The Revolution in Virginia.* Boston, 1916.

Ege, Thompson P. *History and Genealogy of the Ege Family in the United States, 1738–1911.* Harrisburg, Pa., 1911.

English, William H. *Conquest of the Country Northwest of the River Ohio, 1778-83, and Life of George Rogers Clark.* 2 vols. Indianapolis, 1896.

Evans, Emory G. "Planter Indebtedness and the Coming of the Revolution in Virginia." *WMQ,* 3d ser. 19 (1962):511–33.

Ezekiel, Herbert T., and Lichenstein, Gaston. *The History of the Jews of Richmond from 1769 to 1917.* Richmond, 1917.

Flagg, C. A., and Waters, W. O. "Virginia's Soldiers in the Revolution: A Bibliography of Muster and Pay Rolls, Regimental Histories." *VMHB* 19 (1911):402–14; 20 (1912):52–68, 181–94, 267–81; 21 (1913):337–46.

Freeman, Douglas S. *George Washington.* Vols. 1–4. New York, 1949–52.

Gaines, William H., Jr. *Thomas Mann Randolph: Jefferson's Son-in-Law.* Baton Rouge, La., 1966.

Gottschalk, Louis. *Lafayette and the Close of the American Revolution.* Chicago, 1942.

———. *Lafayette between the American and French Revolutions, 1783–89.* Chicago, 1950.

Graham, James. *The Life of General Daniel Morgan of the Virginia Line of the Army of the United States, with Portions of His Correspondence.* New York, 1856.

Greene, George W. *The German Element in the War of American Independence.* New York, 1876.

———. *The Life of Nathanael Greene.* Vol. 3. New York, 1871.

Greene, Jack P. *The Quest for Power: The Lower Houses of Assembly in the Southern Royal Colonies, 1689–1776.* Chapel Hill, N.C., 1963.

Griffith, Lucille. *Virginia House of Burgesses, 1750–1774.* Northport, Ala., 1963.

Grigsby, Hugh B. *The Virginia Convention of 1776.* 1855. Reprint. New York, 1969.

Gwathmey, John H. *Historical Register of Virginians in the Revolution: Soldiers, Sailors, Marines.* Richmond, 1938.

Harrell, Isaac S. *Loyalism in Virginia: Chapters in the Economic History of the Revolution.* 1926. Reprint. New York, 1965.

Hartley, Cecil B. *Life of Major General Henry Lee.* Philadelphia, 1859.

The Harvie Family. Richmond, 1928.

Hatch, Louis D. *The Administration of the American Revolutionary Army.* Harvard Historical Studies, vol. 10. New York, 1904.

Heitman, Francis B. *Historical Register of Officers of the Continental Army during the War of the Revolution, April 1775 to December 1783.* Washington, D.C., 1893.

Herndon, G. Melvin. "George Mathews, Frontier Patriot." *VMHB* 77 (1969):307–28.

Higginbotham, Don. *Daniel Morgan, Revolutionary Rifleman.* Chapel Hill, N.C., 1961.

———. *The War of American Independence: Military Attitudes, Policies, and Practice, 1763–1789.* New York, 1971.

Hocker, Edward W. *The Fighting Parson of the Revolution: General Peter Muhlenberg.* Philadelphia, 1936.

Hume, Ivor N. *1775: Another Part of the Field.* New York, 1966.

Isaac, Rhys. "Evangelical Revolt: The Nature of the Baptists' Challenge to the Traditional Order in Virginia, 1765 to 1775." *WMQ,* 3d ser. 31 (1974):345–68.

Jackson, Luther P. "Virginia Negro Soldiers and Seamen in the American Revolution." *The Journal of Negro History* 27 (1942):247–87.

James, James A. *The Life of George Rogers Clark.* Chicago, 1928.

Johnson, Victor L. *The Administration of the American Commissariat during the Revolutionary War.* Philadelphia, 1941.

Johnston, Henry P. "Christian Febiger." *Magazine of American History* 6 (1881):188–203.

———. *The Yorktown Campaign and the Surrender of Cornwallis, 1781.* New York, 1881.

Kapp, Friedrich. *The Life of Frederick William von Steuben.* New York, 1859.

———. *The Life of John Kalb.* New York, 1884.

Labaree, Harold A. *Decision at the Chesapeake.* New York, 1964.

La Fayette's Second Expedition to Virginia, 1781. Maryland Fund, pub. no. 32. Baltimore, 1891.

Lassiter, Francis R. *Arnold's Invasion of Virginia.* New York, 1901.

Leake, James M. *The Virginia Committee System and the American Revolution.* Johns Hopkins University Studies in Historical and Political Science, ser. 24, no. 1. Baltimore, 1917.

Lee, Henry [Jr.]. *The Campaign of 1781 in the Carolinas.* 1824. Reprint. Chicago, 1962.

Levy, Leonard W. *Jefferson and Civil Liberties: The Darker Side.* Cambridge, Mass., 1963.

Lingley, Charles R. *The Transition in Virginia from Colony to Commonwealth.* Studies in History, Economics, and Public Law. . . . Columbia University, 36 (no. 2). New York, 1910.

Little, John P. *History of Richmond.* Reprinted from *Southern Literary Messenger* [1851–52]. Richmond, 1933.

Lossing, Benson J. *The Pictorial Field-Book of the Revolution.* Vol. 2. New York, 1860.

Lowell, Edward J. *The Hessians and the Other German Auxiliaries of Great Britain in the Revolutionary War.* New York, 1884.

Lutz, Francis E. *Chesterfield: An Old Virginia County*. Richmond, 1954.

McAllister, J. A. *Virginia Militia in the Revolutionary War*. Hot Springs, Va., 1913.

Main, Jackson T. "The One Hundred." *WMQ*, 3d ser. 11 (1954):354–84.

Malone, Dumas. *Jefferson and His Time*. Vol. 1, *Jefferson the Virginian*. Boston, 1948.

Mayo, Bernard. *Myths and Men: Patrick Henry, George Washington, and Thomas Jefferson*. Athens, Ga., 1959.

Mays, David J. *Edmund Pendleton, 1721-1803*. 2 vols. Cambridge, Mass., 1952.

Meade, Robert D. *Patrick Henry*. 2 vols. Philadelphia, 1957, 1969.

Meagher, Margaret. *History of Education in Richmond*. Richmond, 1939.

Metzger, Charles H. *The Prisoner of War in the American Revolution*. Chicago, 1971.

Mitchell, Robert D. "Agricultural Change and the American Revolution: A Virginia Case Study." *Agricultural History* 47 (April 1973):119–32.

Montross, Lynn. *Rag, Tag, and Bobtail: The Story of the Continental Army, 1775–83*. New York, 1952.

Mordecai, Samuel. *Richmond in By-Gone Days—Being Reminiscences of an Old Citizen*. Richmond, 1856.

Morgan, Edmund S. *Virginians at Home: Family Life in the Eighteenth Century*. Williamsburg, Va., 1952.

Morton, W. S. "List of Pensioners in Virginia for the Year 1786." *WMQ*, 2d ser. 15 (1935):395–96.

Moss, Roger W., Jr. "Isaac Zane, Jr.: A 'Quaker for the Times'." *VMHB* 77 (1969):291–306.

Muhlenberg, Henry. *The Life of Major-General Peter Muhlenberg*. Philadelphia, 1849.

Mullin, Gerald E. *Flight and Rebellion: Slave Resistance in Eighteenth-Century Virginia*. New York, 1972.

Naisawald, Louis V. "Robert Howe's Operations in Virginia, 1775–1776." *VMHB* 60 (1952):437–43.

Nelson, William H. *The American Tory*. New York, 1961.

Norvell, Watkins. *Richmond, Virginia: Colonial, Revolutionary, Confederate, and the Present*. n.p., 1896.

"Note on 'Belvidere'." *VMHB* 39 (1931):139–45.

Palmer, John M. *General Von Steuben.* New Haven, 1937.

Peterson, Merrill D. *Thomas Jefferson and the New Nation.* New York, 1970.

Porter, Albert O. *County Government in Virginia: A Legislative History, 1607–1904.* New York, 1947.

Price, Jacob M. "The Rise of Glasgow in the Chesapeake Tobacco Trade, 1707–1775." *WMQ,* 3d ser. 11 (1954):179–99.

Rankin, Hugh F. *Criminal Trial Proceedings in the General Court of Colonial Virginia.* Williamsburg, Va., 1965.

―――. *The North Carolina Continentals.* Chapel Hill, N.C., 1971.

Read, D. B. *The Life and Times of General John Graves Simcoe.* Toronto, 1890.

Reams, Louise A. "Taxation in Virginia during the Revolution." *Richmond College Historical Papers* 2 (1917):43–73.

Report of the Committee on Public Lands. 28th Cong., 1st Sess. 2 May 1844. House Rept. 457.

Richmond, Capital of Virginia: Approaches to Its History. Richmond, 1938. A project of the Virginia Capital Bicentennial Commission, this book contains essays by prominent Richmonders on various topics relating to Richmond.

Richmond Portraits in an Exhibition of Makers of Richmond, 1737–1860. Richmond, 1949.

"Richmond-Randolph Lodge, No. 19: A Historical Sketch." *Virginia Masonic Journal* 23 (February 1929):1–3, 10–11.

Riley, Edward. "Yorktown During the Revolution," pt. 1. *VMHB* 57 (1949):23–43.

Ripley, William Z. *The Financial History of Virginia, 1609–1776.* New York, 1893.

Rosenblatt, Samuel M. "The Significance of Credit in the Tobacco Consignment Trade: A Study of John Norton & Sons, 1768–1775." *WMQ,* 3d ser. 19 (1962):383–99.

Rossiter, Clinton. "Richard Bland: The Whig in America." *WMQ,* 3d ser. 10 (1953):33–79.

Rowland, Kate M. *The Life of George Mason, 1725–92, Including His Speeches, Public Papers, and Correspondence.* 2 vols. New York, 1892.

Russell, John H. *The Free Negro in Virginia, 1619–1865.* Baltimore, 1913.

Scheer, George F., and Rankin, Hugh. *Rebels and Redcoats.* Paperback edition, New York, 1957.

Schmidt, Fredrika T., and Wilhelm, Barbara. "Early Proslavery Petitions in Virginia." *WMQ,* 3d ser. 30 (1973):133–46.

Scott, Arthur P. *Criminal Law in Colonial Virginia.* Chicago, 1930.

Scott, Mary Wingfield. *Houses of Old Richmond.* Richmond, 1941.

Sellers, Charles C. *Benedict Arnold: The Proud Warrior.* New York, 1930.

Shackelford, George W. "Benedict Arnold in Richmond, January, 1781." *VMHB* 60 (1952):591–99.

Smith, Glenn C. "Era of Non-Importation Associations, 1768–73." *WMQ,* 2d ser. 20 (1940):84–98.

Smith, Paul H. *Loyalists and Redcoats: A Study in British Revolutionary Policy.* Chapel Hill, N.C., 1964.

Stanard, Mary N. *Richmond: Its People and Its History.* Philadelphia, 1923.

Stanard, W. G. "Racing in Colonial Virginia." *VMHB* 2 (1895):293–305.

Stedman, Charles. *The History of the Origin, Progress, and Termination of the American War.* 2 vols. London, 1794.

Stewart, Mrs. Catesby Willis. *The Life of Brigadier General William Woodford of the American Revolution.* Richmond, 1973.

Stewart, Robert A. *The History of Virginia's Navy of the Revolution.* Richmond, 1933.

Stowe, Walter H., et al. "The Clergy of the Episcopal Church in 1785." *Historical Magazine of the Protestant Episcopal Church* 20 (1951):243–77.

Sydnor, Charles S. *Gentlemen Freeholders: Political Practices in Washington's Virginia.* Chapel Hill, N.C., 1952.

Swem, Earl G., and Williams, John W. *A Register of the General Assembly of Virginia, 1776–1918, and of the Constitutional Conventions.* Richmond, 1919.

Taliaferro, Grace E. S. *A Story of St. John's Church, 1607–1964.* Richmond, 1968.

Tatè, Thad W. "The Coming of the Revolution in Virginia: Britain's Challenge to Virginia's Ruling Class, 1763–1775." *WMQ,* 3d ser. 19 (1962):323–43.

Tharp, Louise H. *The Baroness and the General.* Boston, 1962.

Thayer, Theodore. *Nathanael Greene: Strategist of the American Revolution.* New York, 1960.

Tower, Charlemagne. *The Marquis de La Fayette in the American Revolution.* Vol. 2. 1894. Reprint. Freeport, N.Y., 1971.

"Two Streams Become One." *Virginia Calvacade* (spring, 1958), pp. 23–29.

Tyler, Lyon G. *Encyclopedia of Virginia Biography.* Vol. 1. New York, 1915.

———. *The Letters and Times of the Tylers.* Vol. 1. Richmond, 1884.

Van Tyne, Claude H. *The Loyalists in the American Revolution.* New York, 1902.

"Virginia Militia in the Revolution." *VMHB* 14 (1907):80–81; 15 (1908):87–92, 186–94.

"Virginia Officers and Men in the Continental Line." *VMHB* 2 (1895):241–58, 357–70.

"Virginia's Soldiers in the Revolution." VMHB 19 (1911):402–14; 20 (1912):52–68, 181–94, 267–81; 21 (1913):52–68, 181–94, 267–81, 337–46.

"Virginia State Troops in the Revolution." *VMHB* 26 (1918):58–69, 182–89, 290–96, 397–400; 27 (1919):62–67, 336–44; 28 (1920):58–64, 247–55, 359–60; 29 (1921):58–64, 439–44; 30 (1922):56–59, 377–84; 31 (1923):326–32; 32 (1924):183–87, 360–64; 34 (1926):259–62; 37 (1929):34–38.

Wallace, Lee A., Jr. "The Battery at Hood's: An Ambitious Fortification Failed to Protect Richmond in the Revolution." *Virginia Calvacade* 23 (1973): 38–46.

Wallace, Willard M. *Traitorous Hero: The Life and Fortunes of Benedict Arnold.* New York, 1954.

Ward, Christopher. *The War of the Revolution.* 2 vols. New York, 1952.

Ward, Harry M. *Department of War, 1781–95.* Pittsburgh, 1961.

Warner, Pauline P. *The County of Henrico, Virginia: A History.* n.p., 1959.

Weddell, Alexander W. *Richmond Virginia in Old Prints, 1737–1887.* Richmond, 1932.

White, Blanche S. *First Baptist Church, Richmond, 1780–1955.* Richmond, 1955.

Wickwire, Franklin, and Wickwire, Mary. *Cornwallis: The American Adventure.* Boston, 1970.

Wildes, Harry E. *Anthony Wayne, Trouble Shooter of the American Revolution.* New York, 1941.

Willcox, William B. "The British Road to Yorktown: A Study in Divided Command." *American Historical Review* 70 (1946):1–35.

_____. *Portrait of a General: Sir Henry Clinton in the War of Independence.* New York, 1964.

Willison, George F. *Patrick Henry and His World.* New York, 1969.

Wirt, William. *The Life of Patrick Henry.* New York, 1903 ed.

Wright, Marcus J. "General Lafayette's Campaign in Virginia, April 1781–October 19, 1781." *Publications of the Southern Historical Association,* 9:234–40, 261–71. Washington, D.C., 1905.

Index